Election 2016

How Donald Trump and the Deplorables
Won and Made Political History

by John Kinsellagh

Table of Contents

Foreword

Your could tell by their faces.

One by one, as key states were called for Trump during the night and the electoral votes tallied inexorably in his favor, the faces of the anchors, commentators and reporters turned ashen, drawn. Shellshocked, they gazed into the camera. When they spoke, there was disbelief in their plaintive voices. Some, spoke in hushed, somber tones, as if they had just been notified that a close family member had died.

Indeed, for many in the media, the atmosphere was appropriately funereal. For those journalists who acted dutifully as members of Hillary's cheerleading squad, their hopes, like hers, had been crushed.

There would be no coronation gala at the Javits Center, the planned festivities, now unceremoniously cancelled. Even though Hillary had already hired the fireworks crew, there would be no multi-colored light display over the Hudson.

Election night 2016, for many, ended with a whimper and not a bang.

In its aftermath, many institutions ruptured. During the election, journalists squandered their credibility by openly colluding with the Clinton campaign and the Democratic Party. They are now forever tainted. The media has become a bona fide opposition party, whose goal is to overturn, in concert with Democrats, the results of the election and drive Trump from office by any means necessary.

The Republican and Democratic parties will never be the same again. The fissures in both parties, long dormant, rose to the surface, widened and split both parties apart. The Democratic Party has completely forsaken what was once the backbone of its coalition: the white working and middle classes. Hard left progressives will now battle with urban minorities, gentry eco-liberals, academics and Hollywood celebrities for control of the Democratic Party.

For the GOP, there will be no going back to business as usual. The election of

Trump slayed Bush Republicanism forever. A lot of new voters were brought into the party and its future will depend on how well the GOP can integrate these disaffected working class voters with its corporate donor and Chamber of Commerce factions. This will be no easy task. There are many exiles in the party who would like to turn the clock back to the 20th century and restore the establishment. Should this happen, the GOP will not survive. Either a new party will be formed or the Republican Party will split off into its new constituent parts.

How did this immense and historical upending of the established political order happen?

Prologue

Donald Trump's stunning victory did not occur in a vacuum. The election of 2016 represented one of those rare events that have occurred in our history where a candidate and the concomitant political environment were perfectly aligned to create an historical moment of great significance. The Trump phenomenon could not have transpired had there not been a widening gulf between the interests and/or policy preferences of elites in the media, academia, as well as government and those of the voters. The country had slowly evolved into a class/cultural based society, split primarily between those clustered in urban enclaves on the two coasts and those who reside in the heartland or flyover country. Trump brilliantly sensed this growing divide, ripe for political exploitation and he rode the wave of disenchantment — completely missed by aloof and incurious elites — all the way to the White House.

Before Trump arrived on the political scene, the whole country was awash in a stifling swamp of political correctness run amok. The speech police were omnipresent and unforgiving to those who didn't conform to the catechism of progressivism in word and deed. Academic institutions birthed new theories and concepts to feed the diversity beast's need for instances of perpetual grievance. "White privilege" was the latest socioeconomic theory birthed on college campuses and implicitly incorporated into the Democratic Party's platform. Any criticism of the extremism expressed by the Black Lives Matters movement was verboten.

During the previous eight years, free speech was under assault. The Obama Administration seemed more interested in what bathrooms transvestites should be allowed to use rather than in the plight of the unemployed in the nation's great heartland. Curt Schilling, the famed Boston Red Sox pitcher and commentator for ESPN, was cashiered by that network for his alleged misconduct in having the audacity to suggest that men should use the men's room and vice versa.

Writing in the *National Interest*, Robert W. Meery described the reaction of many Americans, "But it wasn't clear until Trump's emergence just how much ordinary citizens chafed at this cultural phenomenon in terms of the impact on their own everyday lives. Political correctness has sought, with much success, to narrow the range of political discourse by labeling as illegitimate certain views and thoughts that, just a few years ago, were considered entirely acceptable."[1]

Meery further writes,"Thus, if you believed in secure borders for America, you ran the risk of being labeled a racist or a xenophobe. Same thing if you wondered aloud whether, given the historical antagonism between the West and Islam and the anti-Western fervor of Islamist fundamentalism, it might be best to curb the Muslim inflow into the West. If you harbored traditional views about marriage that, a generation ago, were considered entirely normal by the vast majority of Americans, suddenly you found yourself labeled an extremist or a bigot. If you believed that a civilized society requires a certain respect for law enforcement, you watched in disgust as an assault on the nation's police generated diffidence among officers and their leaders, and contributed to a sudden rise in crime."[2]

For the past thirty years, an inattentive "conservative" party capitulated on every cultural issue forced on the country by the Left, with the result that many young people, schooled by progressive educators, had no conception of the founding fathers vision of a democratic republic. The Republican Party was too immersed in securing tax breaks for corporations and wealthy individuals that they did not perceive nor appreciate the profound change in political philosophy that had occurred in the country. The GOP establishment in fact, embraced, perhaps unwittingly, the lexicon of Left wing ideology that created conditions unfavorable for enactment of its own preferred policies and programs.

It was precisely this refusal to oppose, or at least to speak out against these trends that the rank and file had found the Republican Party wanting. GOP leaders had stood by insouciant, while a tiny elite attempted to ram their cultural preferences down the throats of many Americans who rejected the rabid extremism and agenda of the licentious Left.

There was a growing feeling that the Obama Administration was out of touch with reality. It steadfastly refused to utter the words, "Islamic extremism" to describe attacks on our soil by Muslim fanatics. It preferred to characterize the war on terror by using euphemisms such as "overseas contingency operations." Even when a perpetrator cried out "Allahu Akbar" as he indiscriminately shot at people in Fort Hood, the massacre was described by the Obama Administration as nothing more than an incident of "workplace violence."

The Democratic Party was continuing its inexorable lurch Leftward, increasingly receiving its philosophical direction from the fringes of academia and groups whose primary purpose was grievance-mongering. Paramount among these complaints was the evils of "white supremacy" and "white privilege."

On the nightly news, Americans had witnessed starkly, a surge by illegal immigrants on our porous southern border, a situation encouraged by Obama and completely ignored by the Republican Party elites. As Jim Geraghty of *National Review* wrote, "Recall that in the summer of 2014, tens of thousands of young men, women, and children from El Salvador, Guatemala, and Honduras flooded across our southern border. U.S. Border Patrol officers found that 95 percent of illegal crossers mentioned the rumor that the United States was offering "permisos" (a free pass or permit) to children. This was a misinterpretation of President Obama's 2012 executive order — in which he announced that he would no longer deport young people — and it demonstrated the danger that immigration reform may actually attract more illegal immigrants. Had the GOP helped pass Rubio's plan in 2013, they would have been equally culpable for the tide of young people crossing the border the next year, and that tide would likely have been even larger[3]."

Indeed, in the face of Obama's lawless executive orders, that in one fell swoop, granted without constitutional authorization, citizenship status on an entire class of immigrants, the posture of the Republican Party was one of supreme indifference. Some Illegal immigrants, previously deported multiple times, returned to the U.S. with impunity. The most egregious example of the failure of local governments to enforce the immigration laws was the senseless and completely avoidable murder of Kate Steinle in San Francisco. To those in the heartland, who viewed this spectacle, to add insult to injury, many of these locations declared themselves "sanctuary cities" where federal law was simple nullified. The establishment of the Republican Party expressed blithe indifference. Republican Party primary voters took notice.

The nation's foreign policy was in shambles. Assad, with no fear of retribution from the President of the United States, crossed Obama's famous red line in Syria multiple times with impunity. The president was neither respected nor feared by tyrants and enemies of the country around the world. The Obama Administration had given away the store in the Iran nuclear deal, prepared to subject to humiliation the United States to achieve it. Iran openly defied international maritime laws when it seized an American vessel in international waters and then proceeded to parade the captured soldiers as an act of supreme humiliation to America. This action prompted nary a peep from Barack Obama nor his obsequious, and increasingly clownish Secretary of State, John Kerry.

The fatal shooting of Michael Brown in Ferguson, Missouri in the summer of 2014, created conditions ripe for furthering the myth that there was an epidemic of police shootings against African-American men. As Heather MacDonald observed, "the incident created, "[A] pernicious and blatantly false narrative wholly at odds with the facts/began to be was disseminated/to work its way through the national media, the Congress and the Democratic Party that police officers were targeting black men."Any criticism of the extremism expressed by the Black Lives Matters movement was verboten.

MacDonald further notes, "The highest reaches of American society promulgated these untruths and participated in the mass hysteria. Following a grand jury's decision not to indict a Ferguson, Missouri, police officer for fatally shooting 18-year-old Michael Brown in August (Brown had attacked the officer and tried to grab his gun), President Barack Obama announced that blacks were right to believe that the criminal-justice system was often stacked against them. Obama has travelled around the country since then buttressing that message. Eric Holder escalated a long running theme of his tenure as U.S. Attorney General—that the police routinely engaged in racial profiling and needed federal intervention to police properly.[4]"

After the shooting, thugs ran rampant, many of them bussed from outside Ferguson, where they proceeded to burn down stores and wreak havoc on the town. CNN reporters on the scene nonetheless, constantly referred to the bedlam as "mostly peaceful" demonstrations. Faced with a choice, who were viewers going to believe? CNN reporter Don Lemon or their own lying eyes?

Eric Holder, Obama's Attorney General, made matters worse by using the power of his office to stoke the already incendiary situation by interfering in local judicial proceedings and fanning the flames of racial tension by suggesting that entire police departments were racist and were violating perpetrators civil rights. Across the nation, law enforcement felt that they were under assault.

The country witnessed repeated incidents where journalistic standards were cast aside in order to enhance a preferred progressive narrative. The most egregious example being the University of Virginia rape hoax story published by *Rolling Stone*. Despite numerous warning signs, the magazine continued to pursue the story as if it were true solely because the reporters and editors, given their ideological bias, wanted it to be true. The reporter strained all semblance of due diligence because the story fit perfectly the liberal chimera of a "campus rape" crisis that was purportedly sweeping the nation. The incident diminished further the already low esteem in which many held the media.

Secretary of State, Hillary Clinton lied to the families of those embassy personnel who died in a well planned, coordinated attack against the U.S. Embassy in Benghazi by telling them the tragedy was caused by a defamatory video of Muhammad, when she knew at the time of the attack, that it was a coordinated attack by a terrorist group. President Obama then sent out his national security advisor, Susan Rice, who with breathtaking gall, appeared on every one of the Sunday talk shows and perpetrated this blatant falsehood.

As a perverse indication of how imperial the leviathan federal government had become, many of the richest counties in the nation were now situated in or around Washington, D.C. Over the past decade, salaries for federal workers had escalated obscenely to the point where in some cases they now surpassed the wages and benefits of those in the private sector. After a decades long expansion of the federal government, the nation's capital had now been transformed into a veritable Versailles on the Potomac.

Despite its imperial nature, or perhaps in spite of it, there was a complete lack of accountability for malfeasance and incompetence in the highest levels of the government. The Obama Administration used the IRS, to silence conservative political opponents. Lois Lerner, who was responsible for denying conservative groups tax exempt 501(c)(3) status, operated inside the agency with impunity. When her malfeasance was later discovered, she took the Fifth Amendment and went on administrative leave with full pay. No executive administrators at the Veterans Administration were disciplined for the negligence that led to the deaths of many former servicemen. Indeed, in many instances, these same individuals who were part of the problem received promotions.

Many in the country who witnessed these examples of government corruption and unaccountability were all too eager to support someone who would try and "drain this swamp" of impropriety.

PART ONE
THE REPUBLICANS

CHAPTER ONE

State of the Republican Party

Long before Trump entered the political scene, the Republican Party, as an institution, was broken. Over the course of many years, the GOP had grown dysfunctional. A rift between the elites of the party and its voters developed and with each passing year, this gulf widened. By 2016, the Republican Party no longer represented the interests of its rank and file. The philosophical underpinnings of the party of Lincoln were broken and its leadership increasingly clueless and adrift. After McCain's loss to Obama in 2008, the party was little more than a political platform for the aspirations or policy preferences of its donor class.

There emerged a perverse symbiosis within the GOP where a permanent and fabulously wealthy consultant class, funded by the party's donors, would offer bland, plain vanilla candidates that always lost what could have been winnable presidential elections. A cultural and policy divide between party elites and voters that had been largely inchoate, began to come to the fore. Some of the party's politicians and many of its consultants viewed the conservative wing of the party as "crazies." Many in the upper echelons of the party had more of a cultural connection with their Democratic counterparts than with their own voters.

Commenting on the rise of Trump, Sean Trende, writing in *Real Clear Politics* observed that,

"Trump is a creation of the Republican establishment, which is frankly uncomfortable with many of its own voters, and which mostly seeks to "manage" them. This is a group that looked at the Tea Party revolts of the past decade, looked at the broad field of Republican candidates (many of whom at least had ties to successful Tea Party revolts), and decided that none of these candidates were good enough."[1]

For years, a nascent and insalubrious gap between the party and its voters had been growing. Trump's entry into the presidential race exposed these fissures and upset the status quo. His string of victories created consternation and later, panic among party leaders. In the process of transforming a party badly in need of an infusion of new thinking and new constituents, Trump would banish to the political wilderness some of the establishment favorites, from which they would never return.

Trende noted the growing cultural divide between party elites and voters in some respects is significant:

"this becomes relevant – indeed, I think this is crucial – is that the leadership of the Republican Party and the old conservative movement is, itself, culturally cosmopolitan. I doubt if many top Republican consultants interact with many Young Earth Creationists on a regular basis. Many quietly cheered the Supreme Court's gay marriage decisions. Most of them live in blue megapolises, most come from middle-class families and attended elite institutions, and a great many of them roll their eyes at the various cultural excesses of "the base." There is, in other words, a court/country divide among Republicans."

Trende continues,

"So the Republicans offer up candidates who are from cosmopolitan America, who have their speeches written by speechwriters from cosmopolitan American, who have their images created by consultants from cosmopolitan America, and who develop their issue positions in office buildings located in cosmopolitan America. Then they wonder why the base isn't excited. Say what you will about George W. Bush, but a large part of why he was successful was that he didn't talk like your average D.C. denizen. He was routinely mocked by the press and his own party derided his malapropisms, but he connected with a class of voters that Republicans sure could use these days, in a way that Willard Mitt Romney never could hope to (and without resorting to the demagoguery of Trump)."[2]

Many of these people feel that they have been left out and left behind by the political elites of the country, focused as they are on helping the poor and bringing in immigrants who put downward pressure on wage rates. Few politicians spoke to them or their plight—until Trump.[3]

Every two years the party would promise its voters that it would be true to its core principles: curtail and cut spending; stop the growth of the federal government and battle the hyper-liberal policies of the Democratic Party. As soon as the newly elected politicians reached Washington, voters were told of the difficulties of halting legislation in a divided government. Attempts to foil the licentiousness of the left and the proliferation of its cultural dictates were met by collective shrugs. We can't alienate swing or independent voters was always the refrain. The results of adopting such a policy of laissez-faire on cultural issues so dear to the Left resulted in a nation that was awash in a roiling sea of of political correctness.

The establishment of the Republican Party had done little to halt the corrosive effects these authoritarian progressive policies had on the polity and the right of people to speak freely. Republican voters of all stripes knew their party would do nothing to halt or arrest these disturbing trends. Decades of the "Conservative party" capitulating to the Left on issues of liberty, and religious freedom, sowed the seeds for a Trump candidacy. Although the party fancied itself as the vehicle for implementing conservative goals in terms of the scope and reach of government and the protection of individual liberty, in fact, the policies favored by party elites, in many ways were fundamentally at odds with these underlying principles. The presidency of both Bushes did little to further these goals and the party leaders support for "Comprehensive Immigration Reform", a euphemism for amnesty, was wholly inconsistent with the concept of a sovereign nation-state.

CHAPTER TWO

What does the Republican Party stand for?

Long before Trump burst on the scene in June 2015, the GOP had been in a state of stasis. Party elites and Congressional leaders all accepted the fundamental precepts of party policy and election strategies in force for many years. Despite the fact that he was not the first choice of many Republicans in 2008, John McCain, with the blessing of the establishment, clinched the nomination and then ran a lethargic campaign, whose tempo and posture, in some measure, was dictated by the media, who McCain in many respects viewed as his natural constituency.

The solicitous manner in which McCain conducted his campaign against Barack Obama would lay the foundation for voter disgust and alienation with party elites. The fact that Mitt Romney couldn't defeat his Democratic opponent who was clearly vulnerable, added more fuel to the fire of discontent with the party establishment.

Those who flocked to Trump because of his irreverence on matters of political correctness and the customs of Washington, recognized that during the eight years of the Obama Administration, a rot had overtaken the nation: the ongoing assault by a tiny minority of cultural elites who wanted to transform the entire country. During this time, what has been the response of the purported "conservative" political party? Time and again — taking their cues from the donor class —they simply rolled over and played dead. It was dismaying for long time loyal GOP voters to watch the party's leaders cower before the left-leaning mainstream media. For years the party, especially its consultant class, seemed to relish playing a losing hand: always solicitous of a media elite that despised them, had always despised them and always would despise them.

To view examples of this self-flagellation in action, all one had to do was watch, at random, any one of a multitude of cable TV shows to witness the spectacle of the abject Republican guest worked over by the host, who then proceeded unilaterally, to define the political vocabulary and the permissible parameters of discourse on any given topic, with nary a whimper from the enfeebled Republican guest.

A favorite baiting tactic on which party spokesmen would always be ensnared was the subject of protecting or enforcing our borders. Typically, the liberal host would assert that because GOP voters want a secure Southern border, it necessarily followed that Republicans not only hate all immigrants and are racist, but they also are "anti-immigrant." Few were the instances when the besieged Republican guest would bother to interject and make a distinction between illegal and legal immigration, or bother to expose the linguistic fraud by calling those who broke the law, "undocumented migrants." The Republicans always allowed liberals to define the political vocabulary, unaware of the long-term consequences. What does it say about a political party that its most prominent national spokesmen and/or its candidate for president continually fall prey to this phenomenon?

Every two years, the establishment would make the same tiresome promises to its loyal conservative voters: we will fight Obama at every turn, particularly Obamacare; we will cut spending and work for tax relief; we will stand athwart Obama's extreme left wing agenda. And last but not least, the most fraudulent promise of all, we will secure the border. Among those who planned to vote in the upcoming primaries in 2016, few harbored any illusions that the party would make good on any of these ostensible bedrock principles of the GOP.

In terms of limited government, the party had never been successful in implementing even the slightest reductions in spending or even the rate of spending. Curtailment of federal spending under both Bush Administrations was practically non existent. Indeed, part of the much heralded "compassionate conservatism" of George W. Bush entailed a costly prescription drug plan. Indeed, for many years the GOP participated in pork barrel spending every bit as much as their Democratic counterparts.

On immigration reform, led by the lunacy of John McCain, the Republican Party seemed content to engage in repeated acts of political self-immolation. For years, the establishment had attempted to grant amnesty to some 11 million illegals, in exchange for tenuous promises to "secure" the border. However, the unspoken but ironclad rule accepted by the GOP inner circle, was that these promises were always to be made after the grant of citizenship to millions who had entered the country illegally. In short, Republican voters viewed time and again suicidal attempts by their party to secure a permanent voting bloc for the Democratic Party. Against all the wishes of voters, the party elites continued on their path beholden to the Chamber of Commerce and large corporate donors.

Many voters wondered, why was the establishment so intent on granting citizenship to illegal aliens residing in the country? They could be granted resident status or some other form of standing without giving them the right to vote, which they would undoubtedly exercise in favor of the Democratic Party — an obvious and ineluctable fact that seemed lost on John McCain, the Bushes and the establishment leaders of the Republican Party. As author R.R. Reno astutely noted after Trump's stunning successes during the primaries, "It's long been establishment dogma that there's nothing to be done about immigration. Our economy needs low-cost labor. Native-born Americans are too lazy and spoiled by the safety net to do tough, low-paying jobs (something usually said sotto voce, but sometime out loud). In any event, we're often told the Republican Party needs to adjust to the new multicultural realities, not just in America, but globally.[1]

When stripped bare of its misleading and halfhearted assurances to control our border, the party's position on immigration was indistinguishable from that of the Democrats. This seemed to cause little consternation among members of a party that was purportedly "conservative." The GOP's stance on immigration debased and cheapened the whole concept of citizenship as a fundamental and cherished status for those living in a modern democratic Republic. The party of "conservatism" had clearly demonstrated a complete indifference to one of the core principles of a modern nation-state: that of defined borders that embodies the essence of a sovereign nation.

Other fundamental questions frequently arose in the context of Comprehensive Immigration Reform always favored by donors and their lackeys, the consultant class. First, exactly who would decide our immigration policy? The American people or the Chamber of Commerce? The donor class? The Democratic Party? Whose interests should be paramount in any discussion of immigration reform? The country's own citizens? Those who broke the law? Or, those who will profit from cheap undocumented labor?

On the issue immigration alone, there slowly had evolved a split in the party between the donor class and those Republican voters in the heartland. It had been amply demonstrated by think-tanks that despite the fact that many low-skilled immigrants paid taxes, they were net consumers of social services. Many cities and towns near our southern border had incurred social welfare costs attendant upon the arrival of large numbers of migrants who were destitute and had limited education. Those citizens who had to bear these costs were starting to resent the attitude of the Republican Party which had demonstrated a blissful indifference to those who had to bear the costs and ramifications of unchecked illegal immigration.

Republican politicians who were unaware or utterly indifferent about the nature of today's Democrats had managed the party for too long. The GOP sought comity and congeniality, whereas the Democrats continually engaged in warfare both in the halls of Congress and in the media. John McCain was prone to this blindness on countless occasions during his tenure in the Senate. For McCain, the collegiality and comity of the Senate as an institution was of paramount concern when seeking to bridge partisan divides. Yet his longtime "collegial" colleague Ted Kennedy had no compunction in casting the collegiality of the Senate aside with his vituperative and entirely false character assassination of Robert Bork during his 1987 Senate confirmation hearings. Kennedy's assault on this prominent jurist's character was so offensive and egregious that it spawned a new dictionary term for the lexicon of the late twentieth century: to "Bork."

Kennedy's scorched earth and unprecedented breach of political decorum in 1987 marked the end of "comity" and "collegiality" in the Senate. The politics of personal destruction would rear its ugly head. From that defining moment on, the stewards of the Republican party were clearly unequal to the task at hand in confronting the opposition party and forcefully standing their ground against an onslaught of Democratic Party attacks against individual Republican politicians and the voters who supported them. Some deluded party elders seemed to believed that the media would function as the arbiter of Democratic Party misrepresentations and perfidy. Time and again, the press corps, acting as handmaidens of the Democratic Party showed this was wishful thinking.

The leaders of the party failed to recognize the obvious: for journalists, Republicans were the enemy. The fact that the media had become a wholly-owned subsidiary of the Democratic Party seemed to escape notice by those to whom it should have been self-evident. Currying favor with the broadcast networks was, in the end, always a self-defeating act.

None played this role of useful idiot better than John McCain. A pro-Amnesty stalwart, McCain's natural constituency wasn't the voters of Arizona, but rather, the mainstream media, who delighted in his frequent habit of poking a stick in the eye of conservatives, much to the delight of his cable TV interlocutors. He relished the adulation he received by playing his role as "Maverick"— a bulwark against the crazies of the conservative movement. Many loyal Republican voters who viewed this spectacle wondered out loud how many Democrats criticized members of their own party? The Democrats display enviable message discipline and party loyalty. There is no better example of this than those blue dog Democrats who went down to defeat for their support of Obamacare. Would a Susan Collins ever walk the plank for a Republican president? Nor do Democratic Party consultants openly criticize their party in the same manner as the Republican consultant class —much to the delight of Chris Matthews of MSNBC as well as other cable news commentators and reporters.

As long as the Republican Party was held captive to the donor class, there would continue to be incipient dissatisfaction within the ranks. The principal interests of the donor class has always been tax cuts and cheap illegal immigrant labor. As long as the interests and overriding philosophy of the party was subservient to these uninspiring goals, the more the party itself drifted off into irrelevance, not only for voters dissatisfied with the direction of the Democratic Party, but for those loyal conservatives within the Republican Party.

Those Republicans who occupied leadership positions in Congress were little better than their corporate sponsors in this regard. Party stalwarts could never go beyond communicating in terms of lower taxes, limited government and a robust — and at times — adventurous foreign policy. The sad truth was that for many years the Republican Party lacked a nationally recognized spokesmen or member(s) who could speak with authority and conviction about what the party stood for, where the party was going and why average voters should come on board. All the leaders of the party could ever muster was banal talk about tax cuts and not alienating the Hispanics. There was no public discussion concerning how its proposed policies would benefit blue-collar workers.

The domestic economic effects NAFTA and other trade agreements, put in place by the Clinton Administration had worked their way though the country with the result that huge swaths of middle America were carved out, hollow and distressed economically and culturally. The Republican Party establishment completely missed the groundswell of discontent felt by these economically distressed voters, many of whom had voted for Obama. Many of these lifelong Democrats felt alienated culturally from a party that continuously mocked and deprecated their way of life. These were the new voters who would be up for grabs in this election by virtue of their disgust with cultural and political elites in general and the Democratic Party in particular.

CHAPTER THREE
The Republican Old Guard

Prior to the Election of 2016, the Republican Party as an institution, had become staid, uninspiring and ill-suited to do battle with the modern day Democratic Party and its wholly-owned subsidiary the mainstream media. The image the party projected was that of a country club, whose members may have been pleasant enough, but who were not really attuned to the thoughts, lifestyles and concerns of middle class voters. One of the weaknesses of the party was that its upper echelons were filled with those, who while successful in the private sector, we're wholly ignorant about communicating the values that were under assault by the Democratic Party and its minions in academia and the media.

The Old Guard was just that: an ossified cadre of advisors, consultants, congressional and party leaders who were incapable of thinking outside the box and who convinced themselves the political world had stood still after George H.W. Bush was president. They were unable to anticipate Trump because they were operating in a tight-knit isolated bubble where Republican voters were to be managed and given an ultimatum come every election with the refrain: you may not like our candidate, but who are you going to vote for, the Democrat?

Long the establishment favorite for the 2016 election cycle, Jeb Bush represented the bland, timid type of candidate favored by the Old Guard of the party, which reduced to its essence was: balanced budgets, tax cuts, don't alienate the rising tide of Hispanic voters and at all costs, avoid cultural issues. Trump, unlike those members of the *Ancién Regime* didn't subscribe to this poppycock. Despite expanding the voting base of the Republican Party, he was castigated by many as an heretic. The party, without the slightest reservation or skepticism, wholeheartedly bought into, indeed embraced, the much ballyhooed political theory of the "coalition of the ascendant" endlessly peddled by Democrats, cable TV commentators and political consultants.

This helps explain why the party establishment failed to anticipate Trump and didn't have the vaguest idea of how to respond to his string of primary victories. Comments from party leaders in New Hampshire during the primary season are indicative of an institution that completely misread the mood of its own voters. In January, 2016, Byron York, of the *Washington Examiner*, wrote perhaps the most telling piece of journalism about Trump's campaign in New Hampshire. York talked to the major Republicans in the state, "[and]they didn't know any Trump supporters: As York noted, Most of the politicos in Nashua didn't deny that the polls are what they are. They just explained that they haven't personally encountered evidence that the Trump-dominated polls are accurate. "I don't see it," said one very well-connected state Republican. "I don't feel it. I don't hear it, and I spend part of every day with Republican voters."[1]

York concluded by observing, "The Republican Party has no idea who Trump supporters might be. That may be why the Trump rebellion exists in the first place. Like Pat Buchanan in 1996, Donald Trump's populist, blue-collar-focused campaign carried the Granite State."[2]

Some of the most prominent members of the Old Guard are the consultant class, who for the past several election cycles maintained an incestuous and profitable relationship with the RNC. Win or lose, the same names would usually crop up: Mike Murphy; Steve Schmidt; Stuart Stevens; John Weaver and Rick Wilson. These political strategists all fed off the parasitic relationship with the party establishment. They repeatedly bilked the RNC and its donors — both large and small. They all sang the same old song. They could all be seen on the cable TV and Sunday morning talk show circuit, their appearances ostensibly booked due to their expertise, which was comical, given their dismal track record.

The track record of the consultant class pariahs was dreadful, yet the party continued to hire them. It was a unique and enviable employment relationship where the worse you performed the greater your job security and the more you were paid.

As Matthew Sheffield of *Praxis* sarcastically noted, "Anyone who hurts the Democrats' electoral prospects is dead. Not so, the Republicans. If John Edwards, Ned Lamont, and Bill Bradley were Republicans, they'd have radio shows, TV gigs, and bestselling books." Sheffield continues, "No one gets rich by sabotaging the Democratic Party. But a lot of people get rich off losing races for the Republican Party. […]. For all the mocking that conservatives gave to Bob Shrum, the perennial failure who managed the 2004 Kerry campaign and many other Democratic disappointments, the list of Republican consultants who continue to get paid millions despite their obvious incompetence is far too long.[3] Sheffield presents a sampling of some of the perennial Republican losers who continue to feed at the trough:

> Mike Murphy is the quintessential example of a Republican consultant who should have been laughed out of politics long ago. He's lost campaigns for John McCain, Rick Lazio, Christine Whitman, and Lamar Alexander. He also has the dubious distinction of running one of the most expensive losing state-level campaigns in history, the $177 million failure of Meg Whitman to win the California governor race in 2010. Then again, he probably didn't mind the loss considering that he was siphoning $1.3 million a month from the organization. Murphy's past failures did not seem to have harmed him as he was hired to run the political action committee backing Jeb Bush's doomed-from-the-start bid for the Republican presidential nomination. As would be expected, Murphy managed to spend $130 million before Bush dropped out following his embarrassing loss in South Carolina. Since Bush received only 934,635 votes in three states before withdrawing, this means Murphy literally spent $1,374 for each vote the former Florida governor received.

Sheffield skewers another establishment favorite,

> John Weaver is yet another failure who somehow continues getting work. His list of stinkers is huge, most notably his failed attempts to manage John McCain's presidential campaigns in 2000 and 2007 (he was fired before any votes were cast). In 2012, he advised John Huntsman in his bid to get the GOP presidential nomination. His counsel to the Utah governor was his usual advice of encouraging Republican politicians to start attacking their own party while not offering any real alternative. Shockingly, it didn't work. Like Murphy, his serial failures seem not to have impacted his ability to get work. In the 2016 cycle, he was the campaign manager for Ohio governor John Kasich's quixotic presidential campaign which managed to win only his home state of Ohio.

And saving the best for last, Sheffield exposes the dreadful record of Steve Schmidt,

> Though he's often portrayed as some sort of expert on television, Steve Schmidt isn't exactly someone who's gone from success to success. In 1998, he was the communications director for a botched campaign against California senator Barbara Boxer. One year later, he held the same position for the dull and uninspiring presidential campaign of Lamar Alexander. He managed to help Arnold Schwarzenegger win re-election as governor of California but then returned to his losing ways in 2008 as he helmed the daily operations for the failed John McCain presidential campaign where he recommended Sarah Palin as the vice presidential candidate and thereby removed the strongest reason to vote against Barack Obama, who was at the time a junior senator from Illinois who had been in office for only two years. Yet instead of working to overcome his mistake, Schmidt launched an unprofessional private smear campaign against Palin which harmed McCain even more by undercutting his judgment in the press. Schmidt's catastrophic mismanagement of the McCain campaign seems not to have harmed his ability to continue getting work, something that surprised New York Times reporter Adam

Nagourney who couldn't help but note that he "stands as evidence that there may be little cost to being associated with a losing campaign and a disastrous political misjudgment.[4]

What is astonishing, is that the Republican Party is known, above all else, as the party of business and home of successful entrepreneurs. How members of this elite business club could repeatedly shower astronomical sums and continue to employ the consultant gang that couldn't shoot straight, time and again, is one of the most endearing mysteries of the GOP of the past thirty years. If the Republican Party were forced to compete in the private sector with the same business plan employed repeatedly by the RNC, they would sooner or later be forced to file for bankruptcy.

To add insult to injury, not only did these consultants have dismal track records despite the obscene sums they are paid, but they seemed to consider it sport to attack and demean conservatives. No one excelled in this task of playing Quisling better than the execrable Steve Schmidt—architect of John McCain's defeat in the 2008 election. Schmidt, a longtime Republican consultant and bane in the eyes of the party's conservative voters, had this to say about Trump's popularity and primary victories: "We've seen in this campaign the emergence of this underbelly of American nativism, of white nationalism, the alt-right movement," he says. "If you have any sense of history it's not difficult to look at this and be very disturbed by it. There's always been a question in America of: could it happen here?" Schmidt concludes on a note of cautious optimism, "The one hope is that all the crazy people in the Republican party are older and the crazy people in the Democratic party are younger."[5]

A regular on the hard-left cable channel MSNBC, Schmidt relished criticizing the culturally conservative wing of the party. Much to the delight of his MSNBC host, Schmidt predicted the party's doom if it didn't abide by the "coalition of the ascendant" nonsense and ignore the cultural concerns of GOP voters who simply didn't want their country to evolve into a province of Amsterdam without a fight from the party of purported "conservatism."

At a Conservative Political Action Conference panel in 2013, Democratic party pollster Pat Caddell described the Republican donors reliance on the same consultants who lose as madness. Caddell did not mince words in his characterization of the relationship: "I blame the donors who allow themselves to be played for marks. I blame the people in the grassroots for allowing themselves to be played for suckers," he said. "It's time to stop being marks. It's time to stop being suckers. It's time for you people to get real." In addition, Caddell had harsh words for Stuart Stevens, Mitt Romney's political consultant. "The Romney campaign is the single worst campaign in the history of the United States," Caddell further noted that, "[Chief strategist Stuart] Stevens had as much business running a campaign as I do sprouting wings and flying out of this room."[6] In the 2016 GOP primaries, Stevens, demonstrated his political prowess yet again, with his brilliant prognostication that Trump would drop out of the race before the Iowa caucuses.

Running Off the Same Playbook

After Romney's defeat in 2012, the GOP remained a Bush party in temperament, staffing, outlook and spirit. The policy goals, and direction of the party were firmly in the hands of Bush loyalists, staffers who had either served in the GHW Bush or George W. Bush Administrations. Jeb was the favored nominee in 2016, which indicated that the establishment had every intention of insuring that the party continued to bear the imprimatur of the Bush family. Oblivious to the fact that the country, media and political environment of the nation had changed dramatically since the late 1980's, party elites resided in a time warp. The elites of the party were like the generals who always were fighting the last war. The uninspiring battle cry was, "Fiscally conservative, socially liberal." The delusion of the Republican Party, as shown by the advice its consultants gave two unsuccessful presidential nominees, is the way to win presidential contests is to yield to the left on moral and other trendy issue dear to the heart of a Democratic Party that has consistently been moving leftward over the past two decades. Why would the GOP think that the way to expand its electoral reach would be to emulate a party that has been thoroughly Europeanized and increasingly transformed into a purely bicoastal institution of elites, academics, Hollywood stars, gentry liberals and urban minorities?

After their loss in 2012, leaders of the Republican Party began work on a project that would later be dubbed the "Autopsy Report," a document that analyzed the reasons for the party's loss in 2012 and offered a proscription for the party to be more competitive in the next election cycle. Those who created and drafted the report were predominantly individuals who had worked for either George W. Bush or his father or were longtime and loyal supporters of the Bush family. A sampling of the authors is instructive: Ari Fletcher (former press secretary in the George W. Administration); Sally Bradshaw (longtime Bush loyalist and one of Jeb Bush's key strategists); Mike Murphy (longtime Republican consultant and advisor to both Bush and McCain); Henry Barbour (veteran Mississippi Political operative).

In terms of its underlying theme, the Autopsy report was music to the ears of the party's large individual and corporate donors, who had long subscribed to Bush Republicanism by virtue of their primacy in the candidate selection process and fashioning the party's policy preferences. In either case, the outcome would be the same: an uninspiring Republican who was all to eager to do the bidding of the GOP's donor class.

The report's recommendations incorporated a set of underlying assumptions that were tenuous at best, and utterly specious at worst. The party elders willingly subscribed to the view, trumpeted incessantly by democratic pundits and cable news commentators, that due to demographic changes, the white working class was rapidly becoming extinct and that to survive in a country that was increasingly becoming diverse and non-white, the party needed to appeal to the "coalition of the ascendant."

The authors of the report seemed to think that the inevitability of the coalition of the ascendant was an act of divine providence, when in fact, one of the reasons for the growth of the Hispanic population had been the utter failure of the party to change immigration policy that had for years favored low skilled immigrants from Mexico and Central America. Chain migration and birthright citizenship only guaranteed that the Hispanic population would increase. This had been the immigration policy of the country since Ted Kennedy changed it in 1965. More importantly, the argument that the party needed to soften its stance on illegal immigration in order to pander more to the Hispanic community was wholly inconsistent with the facts.

George W. Bush's capturing 40 percent of the Hispanic vote in the 2004 election, was the high-water mark for the Republican Party. Thereafter, it declined, regardless of how much the party claimed that it supported Comprehensive Immigration Reform. John McCain was the most pro-amnesty Republican who had ever run a presidential campaign and he only received 31 percent of the Hispanic vote. The next establishment candidate, Mitt Romney, did even worse at 27 percent Despite party leaders antipathy towards Trump and their fear that he would leave the party in tatters, he captured 29 percent of the Hispanic vote, better than Romney and almost identical to pro-Amnesty John McCain's share.

Despite the fact that the post-election evidence clearly suggested that Hispanic voters preferred the Democratic Party, the report's authors decided nonetheless to continue aggressively with the party's Hispanic outreach. As Jim Geraghty of *National Review* noted, "the Republican National Committee's official autopsy of what went wrong in 2012, proved to be spectacularly wrong in predicting what the political environment would look like at the end of President Obama's second term.[1]"

But, they repeatedly ceded to the media and Democrats the task of defining the scope of permissible political discourse, including those topics that the Left believed were *prima facie* instances of alleged racism, homophobism, etc., so, too did they willingly adopt, without reservation or skepticism, one of the most cherished political myths of liberals: that the Republican Party was destined to be a rump party in light of the inexorable demographic decline of white voters. It was simply astounding that there wasn't a soul in the party who would have viewed as suspect a theory that was advanced enthusiastically by the opposing party.

Geraghty further observed that, "the RNC report's advocacy for a path to citizenship was a slap in the face to those Republicans who had long been angry about illegal immigration. Businesses big and small made the decision to employ illegal immigrants in violation of the law. A generation of Washington politicians responded with a tacit shrug, even after 9/11."[2] Accordingly, when the party decided to base its election strategy in 2016 on the horribly misguided Autopsy Report, the GOP electorate greeted it with disdain. In part, because the autopsy report in many respects comported well with the philosophy of "compassionate conservatism", the party hierarchy adopted these recommendations enthusiastically and without reservation.

On March 18, 2013, the day the report came out, Trump responded on Twitter that the Republican Party had a death wish. He expanded his critique by stating the, "report was written by the ruling class of consultants who blew the election. "Short on ideas." "Just giving excuses to donors." In terms of the 2016 election, Trump's words would prove to be eerily prescient.

Not one author of the report represented any divergent or opposing views. The report was simply an exercise of former Bush insiders preaching to the choir. In a change election year, the results were predictable: the underlying premises of the Report, so at odds with the mood of the party's voters, was soundly rejected.

In some regards, one could argue that there wasn't a material difference between the policy preferences of Jeb Bush and Hillary Clinton. When one examines Trump's main opponents— Bush and Rubio then, Hillary Clinton now —on the critical issues of immigration (legal and illegal), trade, and Iraq and other military interventions, one finds no substantial differences between them. Both were pro-amnesty advocates and made nary a peep about the concerns of voters (from both parties) about the deleterious effects of illegal immigration. Sure, Bush believed in limited government and Hillary in its expansion, but how limited a government did Bush and the Old Guard truly want.

One only needs to harken back to the days of George W. Bush's 'compassionate conservatism", the prescription drug cost and the inability to curtail the rate of growth in the federal bureaucracy to argue that the Bush family, like their democratic counterparts, had no interest or stomach for the dismantling of the bureaucracy. They might make some symbolic tweaks here and there, but at the end of the day, nothing would have changed.

Jay Cost, writing in *The Weekly Standard* noted that, "By 1994, 60 years of Democratic dominance of the legislature had created an expansive system of interest-group liberalism, whereby Congress distributes largesse to the interest groups that are most able to work the system to their advantage. Promising a 'revolution" in 1994, congressional Republicans have actually strengthened that regime. From farm subsidies to corporate tax giveaways to payouts for the medical services industry to the congressional pork barrel, the list of Republican clients for big government payola is seemingly endless. None of this is consistent with a party that stands for a smaller government administered impartially."[3]

Cost further observed the irony of this for the party of "limited government", "If we believe Burke and Madison, then a party should elevate and manage the public discourse, around principles that advance the general welfare. Nobody honestly believes today's Republican party is capable of this on a national level."[4]

After years of promises not kept in regards to curtailing spending, voters correctly surmised that the Bush faction of the party and the Old Guard was in many ways nothing more than "Democratic lite." What the gurus and exalted campaign consultants in the party failed to realize, was that if you present general election voters with a choice between a Democrat and a Democrat, they will go for the real Democrat every time.

CHAPTER FOUR
Shock and Awe

Since Jeb was a creature of the establishment that produced the post-mortem blueprint for the GOP, he was the natural candidate of the corporate donor class. Jeb hit all the right buttons embedded in the report: a sublime indifference to the effects, fiscal and cultural, of unchecked illegal immigration; tax reform and avoidance of all contentious social/cultural issues.

Bush had amassed a huge war chest through his PAC America Rising. The strategy of his consultants was that this overwhelming sum of money would force other candidates out of the race before they even started. This was the so-called "shock and awe" strategy. Yet, despite the staggering amount of money funding his campaign, Bush never gained traction. What happened?

The election prognosticators of 2016 assumed without question that campaign cash available to a candidate determined whether elections were won or lost. Jeb's consultants believed that the staggering amount of money he had at his disposal would be sufficient to ensure his nomination as the Republican contender. No one would be able to compete with his ability to run political ads at will. And, he had the unquestioned backing and support of the party elites, but more importantly, the money men of the party, who all threw their hats in the ring once he declared his candidacy. It is astonishing to note that this was the identical strategy, pushed by the consultant class, that had been implemented, without success for the past two previous presidential cycles. Apparently, no one noticed.

Bush's policy prescriptions meshed perfectly with the corporate donors and other contributors and the "moderate" wing of the party. Given the undercurrents of disdain for dynastic elites brewing in the electorate, it is astounding why the Old Guard of the party thought that Jeb was the man of the hour. He had the same last name as a president who, when he left office, had very low favorability ratings.

Jeb's advisers were relying on a strategy that by 2015, was outdated. It was based on the same plan that had served the Bush family well in the past: cash, organization and a pliant primary Republican electorate who would ultimately commit, as they had done in the past, to a center-right candidate favored by the establishment. The playbook was a product of long time Bush family loyalists, such as Sally Bradshaw and consultant Mike Murphy, who believed that what had been successful for two previous presidential elections could simply be dusted off and used again now that it was Jeb's turn. Eli Stokol, writing in *Politico* noted that the playbook, "appealed to the Bush family penchant for shock-and-awe strategy. The campaign would commence with six months of fundraising for the Right to Rise super PAC and enough muscle to push aside Mitt Romney. There would be a massive, broad-based organizational effort to plant roots in March states at a time when other campaigns were mired in Iowa and New Hampshire.

The plan outlined Bush's positive, future-focused message with an emphasis on his decade-old record of accomplishment as Florida governor."[1] However, there were serious problems with the plan, as Stokol observed, that were not apparent to its developers, "The plan roundly underestimated threats: Bradshaw, his closest adviser and longtime defender, for example, told at least one campaign aide that Marco Rubio wouldn't challenge Bush.

Besides, Bradshaw and other top advisers believed, it would be next to impossible for someone with so little experience to beat him."[2] One of the plan's fatal flaws as Stokol further observed was that the Bush team, "thought there was going to be much more reverence and respect for the fact that Jeb Bush, a Bush, was getting into the race," said one Florida-based supporter, an alumnus of Bush's gubernatorial campaigns and former staffer. "When they got Romney to step aside, they figured everyone else would too."[3]

What the shock and awe strategy could never anticipate was the substantial amount of free media Trump was able to secure through the primaries. Because of his controversial statements and highly unorthodox campaign style, Trump was good for business and the cable channels responded accordingly with non-stop round the clock coverage. What Jeb was prepared to spend millions for, Trump was getting for free. Trump was able to render Mike Murphy's entire media buy strategy totally ineffective and obsolete in the 2016 election cycle.

The Rip Van Winkle of the 2016 Election Cycle

Jeb Bush and the Republican Party establishment to which he was indelibly wedded, were both creatures of a political environment that by 2015, had long since passed. The last time Jeb Bush had run a competitive political campaign was in 1998. Yet by 2015, the political, media and foreign policy worlds had changed dramatically. The explosive growth of the internet and its impact on the fracturing and fragmentation of the major broadcast networks meant that no longer would a small band of intellectuals carry a disproportionate sway of the nominating process.

Into this maelstrom stepped Jeb Bush, the Rip Van Winkle of the 2016 election cycle, unprepared for the rigors the new era had imposed on those who had their eyes on the prize of the Republican Party's presidential nomination. It was a mystery why the party elite entertained the notion that by virtue of his last name, he would be a shoo-in as the presumptive favorite, and that he had the best chance to defeat Hillary in the general election.

His brother George W., left office an unpopular president who had presided over an unpopular war in the later stages of his administration and who was at the helm at the beginning of the great economic meltdown of 2008. The idea of nominating the brother of a former president, the memory of which for many Americans was still toxic, was utterly mystifying. Bushism was still the official philosophy for elites within the Republican Party before Jeb entered the race. Only those conjoined to the Bushes by virtue of their prior association with George W. or his father, could earnestly believe that Jeb would be a superlative and implacable candidate.

This conviction was an excellent example of the cloistered groupthink that prevailed within the upper echelons of the party. Some of his comments on the campaign trail were indicative of a candidate who was hopelessly out of step with the times.

On July 31, 2015, Bush made the odd proclamation that, "The climate is changing; I don't think anybody can argue it's not." Lest there be any doubt as to whether he was equivocating, Bush added, "Human activity has contributed to it," Bush said in an email interview with Bloomberg BNA.[1] Jeb and his advisors may have thought that they would be able to curry favor with the media by virtue of his contrarian position to the majority of voters in his party.

Did it not occur to him or his campaign advisors that this was precisely the Democrats position on the global warming scientific hoax. After years of having been debunked and discredited, here he was in accord with the global warming hysteria, a position that was anathema to many in the party. Jeb's position also made him a useful idiot for the Democrats and the media, as they used his belief as an issue to drive a wedge between members of the party.

Had Jeb been more attuned to the 2015 media environment, he would have known that although journalists might have given him favorable coverage in the primary because his positions on some issues mirrored liberal commentators cherished beliefs, but in the general, they would savage him in much the same manner as they had played McCain for a fool in 2008.

In short, Jeb and his advisors unimaginative strategy amounted to little more than business as usual from an establishment that had lost the White House twice already. In many ways Jeb's advisors thought he could run as the natural successor to his brother's presidency. Indeed, many of his policy prescriptions came from the same page as George W's "compassionate conservatism" philosophy.

Tim Alberta of *National Review* described how the establishment favorite Bush, was a mismatch for the times, "Bush fatigue aside, the GOP had shifted rightward in the aftermath of George W.'s presidency, when Jeb himself was out of office and detached from the ideological palpitations of the base. Rubio, ideologically pragmatic at his core, had risen with the tea-party movement and was comfortable riding the electorate's rightward waves. Bush was not: He stubbornly clung to unpopular positions on Common Core and immigration reform, and when he was criticized, famously responded by saying a Republican must be willing to 'lose the primary to win the general.'"[2]

Alberta continues, "It made sense to the old Republican guard, even as it rendered Bush obviously out-of-step with the modern party." Bob Dole was one of those establishment leaders who was flabbergasted, "My view is that Jeb is the best qualified, he's been tested, he dealt with eight hurricanes and tropical storms in 16 months in Florida, he has a very good record as governor, he made over 8,000 appointments and nearly half for women, not just secretarial but in prominent jobs," "I don't know. I just wish people would listen."[3] "There was a time and place, probably a decade ago while his brother was still in office, when he was a very good national candidate," said Reed Galen, a Republican strategist and an alumnus of George W. Bush's administration and presidential campaigns. "I wouldn't say Jeb Bush is out of step with the country," Galen added. "I would say the country is out of step with Jeb Bush."[4]

The longtime Bush family advisors, including those running his campaign, deviated little from their campaign playbook, which was highly influenced by the autopsy report, whose authors included some of the same folks like longtime Bush loyalist, Sally Bradshaw, who unwittingly would write the post-mortem for the establishment in the Election 2016 cycle. There was no fresh blood and hence no fresh thinking. These advisors were locked in a time warp using the same tools in use when George H. W. Bush was president almost two decades ago.

Base, Get in Line

In the 2016 election cycle, Jeb's candidacy was symptomatic of the mismatch between the interests of party elites, donors, consultants and pundits and the mood of the primary electorate. Republican voters had previously elected two Bushes to the presidency and there was a sense that neither Bush 41 nor Bush 43 had lived up to conservative ideals; indeed, the later had increased spending and the former became renowned for his "read my lips"epithet. At the end of the reign of two Bush presidencies, many voters had seen their incomes stagnate, the economy worsen, and under Obama, witnessed complete and utter chaos at the country's Southern border. By 2016, not only was Jeb viewed with disdain by primary voters, but the Republican Party itself, as currently constituted, was as well.

From the moment he entered the race, Jeb Bush didn't even pretend to pay deference to the conservative base of the party. He made the odd proclamation that he would have to lose the primary in order to win the general election, which was code for his intention to ignore his party's more conservative voters. His consultants, supporters and wise men of the party said, that should he decide to run, he would instantly be the putative favorite. His entry into the race would be a "game-changer."

Why these wise men and women of the party believed the republican primary electorate would embrace someone who had been absent from the national stage for almost two decades is bewildering. The voters of the Republican Party would be presented again with another candidate selected by the Old Guard and the corporate donors. They claimed Jeb had the best chance to defeat Hillary, so conservative voters, were told once again to get on board —as they had been told with the candidacies of McCain and Romney.

However, in 2016, for the first time in decades, Republican primary voters were offered a clear choice and they exercised it with a vengeance.

CHAPTER FIVE
Trump's Announcement

It was against a backdrop of what many Americans viewed as troubling signs of national decline, intentionally accelerated by Obama and his hard-left liberal cohorts, that a brash, real-estate billionaire and former reality TV star entered the political fray. When Trump descended down the gold plated escalator to the lobby of his signature Trump Towers building in downtown Manhattan on June 16, 2015 to announce his candidacy for the Presidency, few in the political world could foresee that he would set in motion an election season unlike any other in recent American political history.

Trump took to the podium behind the backdrop of a red pin-strip sign reading "Trump — Make America Great Again," his announcement was broadcast real-time to the nation on television and via live-streaming Internet by the dozens of media outlets competing for the space in front of the podium— all framed against a blue-draped background lined with a row of American flags.[1]

Trump cited many reasons for America's relative decline and he spoke in broad conceptual themes that were easily understood and framed towards the issue of changing policies to make America Great Again. There was no double speak, no discussion of the minutiae of policy details. Trump spoke in simple yet forceful phrases with which many disaffected voters could identify. He did not read from a teleprompter nor any written notes. Much of what the had to say was impromptu, but nonetheless delivered with conviction. In fact, Trump confirmed to the AP the day after his announcement, that his forty-five-minute campaign kickoff speech was not rehearsed. "I did it with no notes, no teleprompter. I like going off-script a little bit," Trump said. "I meant everything I said, and I think a lot of it resonated with different groups of people."[2]

At one point during the speech, Trump expressed his hard line on illegal immigration: "The U.S. has become a dumping ground for everybody else's problems," he said. "When Mexico sends its people, they're not sending their best. They're not sending you. They're sending people that have lots of problems, and they're bringing those problems with us. They're bringing drugs. They're bringing crime. They're rapists. And some, I assume, are good people."[3] Many establishment Republicans found these comments indelicate and Trump's statements would form the basis for sustained media attacks against him.

His acceptance speech was slipshod, shoot from the hip, ad libbed. Though he did have policy issues to present, he did it his way, in an inelegant, rambling, indecorous manner. This speech would set the tone for the remainder of his candidacy. Trump's campaign statements would continue to be brash and forthright; he would not temper nor change his rhetoric to please the media gatekeepers.

The media fired its first shot across Trump's bow shortly after his announcement. The reaction was swift and unforgiving. The talking heads had a field day: Pundits and elites from both political parties greeted the announcement with derision and disdain. He was mercilessly mocked on the cable TV shows and relegated to the sidelines as a showman and clown — perhaps good for the ratings due to the entertainment value, but certainly a candidacy not to be taken seriously.

Minutes after Trump finished with his announcement, CNN commentator S. E. Cupp dismissed it as "a rambling mess of a speech...I was howling. Howling." On MSNBC, host Andrea Mitchell snootily asked the former Democratic Governor of Pennsylvania Ed Rendell: "Do you have any doubt that this is anything more than a carnival show?" The opinion of Most other commentators, both liberal and conservative, were identical. Long-time GOP consultant Steve Schmidt admitted to "laughing out loud" while listening to clips of Trump's speech.[4]

After Trump's speech, *New York Times* reporter, Alexander Burns wrote that, "in the 2000 and 2012 elections, Trump had "hyped up the possibility of seeking the White House before abandoning the idea," suggesting that once again, Trump might only be seeking publicity, in yet another presidential campaign where he could be expected to pull out once the serious, professional politicians took command of the race. Burns ridiculed Trump's policy positions, writing, "Mr. Trump's policy views can be just as provocative as his demeanor. On Tuesday, he vowed to build a 'great wall' on the Mexican border to keep out rapists and other criminals, who he said were sneaking into the United States in droves."[5]

Trump had indeed run as a candidate in the last Republican presidential primary in 2000 and flirted with the idea again in 2012. At that time, he had little to recommend himself as a serious candidate. In short, based on his previous forays into presidential contests, he had given political commentators no indication that he was anything more than a brief flash in the pan in the current election cycle. Perhaps that is one of the reasons political analysts failed to take him seriously. Is it any wonder that these self-same pundits greeted his third entry into the rough and tumble world of presidential electioneering with the same levity. Little did the political world know that this time, the past would not be prologue.

Trump Attacks Political Correctness

Shortly after entering the race, Trump immediately began attacking many sacred cows of the Left and the media with a vengeance. The moment Trump entered the race commentators and reporters excoriated him for the infelicitous way he attacked, openly and without remorse, many of the sacrosanct tenets of liberalism.

Trump also rejected outright the long-held strictures that governed the scope of permissible conduct during presidential campaigns that the Mainstream media-democratic party-complex had established and always used to great effect for years against previous complacent Republican candidates. In past elections, Republican nominees always approached journalists with trepidation — concerned primarily with not rocking the boat, or fearful of accusations that they were insensitive to minorities, callous, racist, mean and nasty.

Tump didn't care one whit what the media thought of him or his message.

Trump's frontal assault on political correctness was an enormous factor in securing his victories, both in the Republican primaries and ultimately, in the general election. Unlike the storied and handsomely paid Republican consultants, who had overseen the disastrous two prior election contests, Trump was the only Republican who understood clearly at the beginning of the race that no matter what a Republican candidate said on the campaign trail, the media was always going to be hostile and critical when it came time to square off against the Democrat.

The one Republican who failed to appreciate this iron law of Republican / media relations more than anyone else was John McCain. During the 2007-2008 primary race, McCain particularly relished his role as the "Maverick," poking a stick in the eye of conservatives — much to the delight of the Mainstream Media whom he courted assiduously. As soon as McCain entered the general election against Obama, he was assaulted by the very same pundits and commentators in the media who had so recently praised him for his willingness to break from conservative orthodoxy. In this regard, Trump shredded the conventional wisdom of party elites and rewrote the playbook for Republicans presidential candidates.

Trump came out of the box swinging. He immediately attacked long-held principles cherished by the Old Guard. One such inviolate rule was speaking out against the Iraq War initiated and managed by George W. Bush. Trump had no compunction in casting aside an unwritten, but nonetheless widely accepted rule that criticism of George W. Bush's disastrous mismanagement of the Iraq War was off limits. This was due in part to the fact that the RNC was staffed disproportionately with holdovers from both Bush Administrations.

Even though Bush was gone for eight years, memories still lingered and the prosecution of that War was one of the reasons Bush had subterranean approval ratings when he left office. Republicans still bore the fallout from those foreign policy disasters, but neither McCain nor Romney criticized, nor attempted to distance themselves in any way from the foreign policy goals of the Bush Administration, most notably the idea of spreading democracy in the Middle East as a means for insuring stability in the region. And, there can be little doubt that they paid a price, however small, with the electorate for their unwillingness to engage in contrition, or criticism. In fact, the foreign policy goals of the Republican Party had changed little since 2008. Many of the establishment foreign policy apartchnicks were veterans of either the GHW or George W. Bush Administrations.

Tump was the first to break from this mold and he did it in a forceful and blunt manner that stunned many foreign policy gurus of the Old Guard. As Ramesh Ponnuru of *National Review* noted, "But it is not necessary to embrace a conspiracy theory to see that the Iraq War was a mistake, and one reason Trump was able to get away with his remarks is that too many other Republicans were unwilling to acknowledge that mistake forthrightly. More than most Republicans, too, Trump advertises his reluctance to spend blood and treasure on overseas conflicts where America does not have vital interests at stake. The public wants that reassurance from Republicans, and it is right to want it; conservatives should give it."[1]

Another bulwark of establishment domestic policy was their steadfast embrace, despite it unpopularity, of Comprehensive Immigration Reform as a "solution" to the problems of unchecked migration at our Southern border. This was an essential component of the Autopsy Report and is an example of the vast gulf between the wishes or preferences of GOP voters and elites and donors of the party.

Trump's immediate call to build a wall on the southern border sparked the ire of Old Guard Republicans. True to form, as an Establishment Republican, John McCain wasted no time in attacking those who would question the wisdom of catering to Hispanics through the political flim flam of Comprehensive Immigration Reform. "The circus currently surrounding the debate over illegal immigration sows division within our country and damages the Republican Party," McCain, the party's presidential nominee in 2008, said in a statement. McCain added that "if the Republican nominee for president does not support comprehensive immigration reform and border security policy, we have no chance of defeating Hillary Clinton and winning the White House in 2016."[2]

McCain's comments came straight from the Autopsy playbook. Republican voters had come to loathe the concept of "Comprehensive Immigration Reform" as nothing more than a fraudulent boondoggle that did nothing to secure the border but contained lots of goodies for the GOP's corporate donors and the Chamber of Commerce. Here was McCain, in 2015 still serving up the same old stew and philosophy that had done nothing to secure the border nor stem the tide of illegal crossings on the nation's Southern border. Imagine to these voters what a breath of fresh air Trump must have been when he rejected the Establishment conventional wisdom.

Trump Sets His Own Rules

Trump's unorthodox style and assault on conventional norms of political behavior, is one of the reasons that he was so singularly effective in offending the sensibilities of the media. When Trump burst on the scene in June, 2015, they were wholly unprepared for the show that awaited them from a man, who not only was a successful real estate developer, but who also was a consummate entertainer. Trump was not a politician, nor an attorney or a Washington insider: he was the consummate outsider, who had his own set of rules, his own way of speaking and his own unique way of dealing with the press.

Trump was not a product of Yale or Harvard and the social circles in which many of the political and media elites travelled, but rather, a product of Queens and the rough and tumble of the New York City commercial real estate business. He was brash, indelicate, and unschooled in the ways of Washington political-speak. As such, many in the chattering classes considered his unwillingness to conform to Beltway traditions a fatal character defect that would inevitably doom his candidacy. No one liked Trump's plain, forthright and wholly unscripted way of speaking and delivering his message except those who voted. One of the most important tell-tale, signs missed by political analysts and commentators during this election was that after years of listening to glib, focus group tested, poll driven and insincere discourse from consultant-schooled politicians from both parties, Trump's supporters found his direct, unpretentious and unadorned method of speaking not only refreshing, but welcome.

Even though their expectations for Trump were low, reporters and commentators believed that he would not breach the etiquette and unwritten rules by which all candidates were bound. In this sense, the media was stunned by Trump because he was unlike any other Republican they had ever encountered. Trump made it clear that he wasn't going to follow the suffocating dictates of political correctness that had all but destroyed political discourse in the nation.

Trump correctly sensed what no other Republican candidate could and that was that many in the working classes who didn't live in the cosmopolitan urban enclaves were reluctant to air their true political and cultural beliefs for the not unwarranted fear that they would be stigmatize as racists, homophobes, etc. Instead of tempering his rhetoric, as many pundits had suggested, instead of staying within the permissible parameters of political discourse defined and enforced by the media, after his announcement, Trump continued to speak his mind and that of many others, when he assailed directly and forcefully the shibboleths of the Left.

When a Republican candidate makes a controversial statement, or more accurately, refuses to abide by or deviates from politically correct stands, reporters and commentators always ask the candidate to retract his statement. The second prong of this well-established tactic is to ask other Republicans candidates if they will criticize or condemn the statement made by the candidate. This song and dance never works out well for Republicans, yet they continue to play the media's game year in and year out.

Trump didn't play along with this ruse. Despite outrage from journalists and commentators over his comments that crime and drugs follow migrants coming across the border from Mexico, Trump stood his ground. in an interview with US Weekly magazine, on June 26, 2015, he refused to retract his earlier statement."There is nothing to apologize for. Everything I said is correct. People are flowing through the borders and we have no idea who they are, where they're coming from. They're not only coming from Mexico, they're coming from all over South America and the world." When CNN host Jake Tapper noted that the Mexican government called Trump's comments prejudicial and absurd, Trump didn't try walk back his statement but instead responded, "Mexico has not treated us well. Mexico treats us as though we are stupid people, which of course our leaders are. I don't blame them. China's even worse."

When fellow Republicans, in lockstep with commentators, criticized Trump for his indecorous remarks about illegal immigrants from Mexico, Trump merely shrugged it off. When Rubio called Trump's comments about Mexicans "offensive, inaccurate and divisive."what was Trump's response? After Mexican illegal immigrant Francisco Sanchez apparently killed 32-year-old Kathryn Steinle in San Francisco in a random attack Wednesday, Trump sent a direct tweet to Rubio:"What do you say to the family of Kathryn Steinle in CA who was viciously killed b/c we can't secure our border? Stand up for US," Trump tweeted.

Federal officials said local authorities repeatedly released Sanchez, who was in their custody as recently as this spring. In the face of this senseless tragedy House Majority Leader Kevin McCarthy, could muster only a lame "there is a role" for the House to play in the face of this senseless tragedy House Majority Leader Kevin McCarthy, could muster only a lame "there is a role" for the House to play in response to Steinle's shooting. "You could hear from Congress."

That following Saturday, Trump assailed Rubio again, saying he was "weak on immigration" and that fellow GOP White House candidate and former Texas Gov. Rick Perry "could have done a lot more."

Rank and file Republican voters were clearly with Trump on the issue of illegal immigration and many must have felt glee as Trump stated the obvious: that Rubio was an opportunistic politician who had flip-flopped on this issue. Many conservative voters who helped elect Rubio to the Senate had bitter feelings and felt betrayed by Rubio's surrender to the Chamber of Commerce wing of the party once he had his eyes on a presidential run.

Trump Confronts Media

During the election, the media was happy to play along with Trump's antics and give him free air time because doing so greatly enhanced their ratings. The networks saw this as a prudent and profitable strategy because they all knew that Trump didn't stand a chance of winning; he was going to lose and lose badly. There was no harm then in humoring him during the primaries and ultimately, the general election contest against Hillary, because they would make him look like a fool and fulfill their predestined role, as official communications organ for the Democratic Party, in facilitating Hillary's ascent to the presidency.

Unlike leaders in the Republican Party, Trump was shrewd enough to realize how tired people were of listening to the latest proclamations of progressives concerning certain speech they deemed offensive and certain behavior — however innocuous — they deemed "hateful." He had his finger on the pulse of Middle America and no one else did.

Trump had no respect for reporters who tried to shame him for his unforgivable sin of failing to talk in "liberal speak." Trump made it clear early on in the race, that he would not be cowed by their criticism of his failure to abide by the unwritten rules of conduct for presidential contestants. This drove reporters and commentators crazy.

Trump deliciously sparred with one reporter in New Hampshire who didn't care for Trump's forthright manner of characterizing children born in this country to illegal immigrant parents as "anchor babies." Fox News described the exchange:

> At a town hall event in New Hampshire yesterday, a reporter challenged Donald Trump on his repeated use of the term "anchor baby."
>
> The reporter asked Trump if he is aware that the term is "offensive" and "hurtful."
>
> "You mean it's not politically correct and yet everybody uses it? Ya know what? Give me a different term," he shot back.

* * *

The reporter suggested he modify his language and instead say "American-born children of undocumented immigrants."

"You want me to say that? No, I'll use the word anchor baby," Trump said, as the reporter tried to interject again.

"Excuse me. I'll use the word anchor baby," he concluded before moving on to another question.[1]

Trump cast this implicit agreement to the wind. He openly chastised reporters on the campaign trail and attacked the cable TV networks who assailed him for deviating from norms of political correctness. He had Univision anchor Jorge Ramos physically removed from one of his press conferences for infraction of the rules for asking questions. Trump, most notably, was unforgiving in his criticism of CNN, which had now, through its openly biased coverage of the race, become the unofficial media cheerleaders for the Hillary Clinton campaign.

What many journalists referred to as Trump's "controversial statements," were nothing more than his refusal to engage in the fraudulent habit of speaking in euphemisms in order to describe unpleasant realities, that if characterized properly and without blandishments, might subject the media's preferred policy positions to heightened scrutiny by the public. Trump was a novelty on the campaign trail because he called things exactly what they were and when his plain and accurate depictions clashed with journalists lexicon in support of their preferred narrative, he was castigated as "divisive" and controversial.

CHAPTER SIX

The Republican Race

At the end of August, 2015, Trump led the pack of GOP hopefuls in the polls. Although this should have been a cause of consternation within the Bush Camp, the belief was that early polling numbers reflected Trump's role as nothing more than a novelty candidate and that when it came time for GOP voters to get serious, the party faithful would come to their senses, close ranks and dutifully support the establishment candidate, as they had done so many times in the past. The most telling indication that Bush Republicans were so out of touch with the party's voters was their not unreasonable belief that the plebeians would once again do as they were told by the party elders, because they had no other choices. Trump provided disillusioned GOP primary voters with a vehicle with which to give the Old Guard the giant middle finger. Unsurprisingly, the Bush campaign never saw it coming.

Nonetheless, most political analysts and commentators viewed Trump as a comet that would burn out quickly. Here is what Jay Cost of *The Weekly Standard* said about the prospect of Trump winning the nomination: " Donald Trump is not going to be the next nominee of the Republican party. The flamboyant businessman has made billions in real estate, but politics is another matter. He manifestly lacks the temperament to be president, and his conversion to the Republican party is of recent vintage. As the field narrows, and voters look closely at the other candidates, Trump will fade.

Nope—not gonna happen."[1]

Trump Rises

Although Bush was viewed as the favorite shortly after he had announced, Trump immediately began to assail his front-runner status. By October 23, 2015, Jeb was down significantly in the polls only three months from the first primary. In October, the Bush campaign slashed the payroll and made other changes. Despite the fact that all the pundits, experts and Republican consultants had declared that another Trump outburst or indelicate campaign statement would terminate his candidacy, Trump continued to deliver his firebrand, brash, hard hitting and unapologetic attacks on many of the inviolate policy preferences of the Republican establishment.

One of the most significant factors responsible for Trump's meteoric rise in the Republican race is that of all the candidates in the crowded field, he was the only one who addressed the issue of illegal immigration forcefully and unequivocally. As Trump correctly noted at the first Republican presidential debate on August 6, 2015, "This was not a subject that was on anybody's mind until I brought it up at my announcement."

His infelicitous comments at his announcement speech about the characteristics of some of those crossing the border from Mexico en masse, incurred the wrath of the liberal press and many sanctimonious Republicans. Trump was the first Republican candidate to expose party's pretend reform proposals for securing the border. Although Establishment candidates always talked tough about border enforcement during elections, next to nothing was done to halt the waves of illegals pouring across the border from Mexico and Central America.

As Mark Steyn correctly observed, in terms of their posture on illegal immigration, there wasn't much substantive difference between the Republican and Democratic Parties, "[t]here is a cozy bipartisan consensus between the Democrat Party and the Donor Party that untrammeled mass unskilled immigration now and forever is a good thing. The Dems get voters, the Donors get cheap labor. The Dems have the better deal, but over on the GOP side the Stupid Party is too stupid to realize that suicide in slow motion leads to the same place as one swift sure slice from Isis."[1]

Trump took the fight to Hillary early during the course of the Republican primaries. On July 15, 2015 he boldly attacked Hillary Clinton, the Democratic contender who at that time enjoyed the highest approval ratings of any candidate in either party. "Easily, she's the worst Secretary of State in the history of our country." Trump said, "She's going to be beaten and I'm the one to beat her."[2] Can anyone imagine a Mitt Romney, a John McCain or a Jeb Bush uttering these words?

In December, 2015, Trump opened up on Hillary with both barrels, strongly condemning her covert, surreptitious and illegal private email communication system, and as a preemptive strike, he criticized Bill Clinton's treatment of women.

As Roger Stone noted, the Clintons weren't dealing with a traditional Republican candidate, "Trump ended 2015 with a flurry of emails pushing back against Hillary Clinton's attacks charging Trump with sexism in his relationships with women. "She's playing that woman's card left and right … Frankly if she didn't, she'd do very poorly," Trump said on CNN. He then turned his sights on Bill Clinton, with another tweet that read, "Hillary Clinton has announced that she is letting her husband out to campaign, but he's demonstrated a penchant for sexism, so inappropriate!" Then, on December 28, 2015, Trump capped off his Twitter attack on the Clintons by tweeting the following: "If Hillary thinks she can unleash her husband, with his terrible record of women."[3]

By his comments, Trump signaled to the media as well as to the Clinton campaign, that there was a new Sheriff in town who would not be bound and encumbered by any explicit or implicit rules of political conduct imposed by the media on Republicans.

Jeb Struggles

While Trump was beginning his unforeseen rise, the fortunes of the anointed candidate of the establishment were starting to diminish, even before the party had held its first primary. Although he had enjoyed the status as frontrunner when he put out feelers about running in 2014, and polled in the mid teens throughout the summer, beginning in late September, 2015, Bush's poll numbers started to drop to the single digits.

On August 6, 2015, Donald Trump surprisingly led a fractured GOP primary field of contenders in the polls. A CBS poll showed Trump at 24 percent leading Jeb Bush, who was at 13 percent, followed by Scott Walker at 10 percent. "Trump leads among a wide array of Republican primary voters," CBS News noted, going into the first debate in Cleveland. "He appears to have tapped into public anger toward Washington: he holds a large lead among Republican primary voters who say they are angry. And 79 percent think Trump says what he believes, rather than what people want to hear, far higher than the other candidates tested."[1]

Bush's fortunes continued to decline precipitously. In late October, 2015, a Bloomberg poll had Bush in fifth place in Iowa and a distant third in New Hampshire. While Bush had polled in the mid teens nationally throughout much of the summer and into the early fall, his numbers declined sharply in late September and early October. By the time of the Colorado debate on October 28, he had sunk to the single digits, where he would spend the remainder of his campaign.

National Review noted that, "Suddenly frantic, his donors, friends, and allies exchanged flurries of doomsday e-mails in the aftermath of the Colorado disaster. With another debate just around the corner in Wisconsin, they worried about his capacity to right the ship. The candidate, sensing that his allies were losing confidence, reluctantly hired famed Fox News media coach Jon Kraushar to help him refine his presentation. And in the run-up to the Wisconsin debate, he dutifully conceded to one audience after another that "I have to get better.""[2]

But Bush's closest allies were beginning to accept the reality that he simply wouldn't. "Debates do not play to his strength," Jim Towey, the president of Ave Maria University in Florida and one of Bush's closest personal friends, said on the eve of the Wisconsin debate. "But I think he's going to be just fine — he'll benefit from the expectations not being that high." Despite Trump's precipitous rise in the polls, establishment gurus continued to make fools of themselves. Stuart Stevens, former campaign manager for Romney's failed 2012 presidential bid, was certain the Trump would drop out before Iowa.

Although party insiders believed Jeb was a sure thing, Bush went into the race with handicaps that his strategists, all who were members of the Old Guard, could not perceive. As Michael Bender and Mark Halperin noted, "Analysts and rival campaigns will view the changes as a desperate act, perhaps the last one, of a man whose campaign has dropped in the polls in recent months and has remained mired in the middle of a crowded field despite a month-long blitz of friendly television ads. None of the changes deal directly with what even many of Bush's supporters say is his main challenge: The burden of trying to convince voters hungry for change to choose a man whose father and brother both served as president.[3]"

As *Politico* noted after Jeb's blowout loss in the the Iowa caucuses, "the bar was low for Jeb Bush's finish in Monday's Iowa caucus. He failed to clear it anyway. After a stunning defeat that landed him in sixth place with just 2.8 percent of the vote, Bush's campaign is now directing top aides and surrogates to highlight the lack of emphasis the one-time front-runner placed on the state – and to make the case that he has far higher expectations in New Hampshire. "The real race for the nomination begins on February 9th in New Hampshire," the campaign wrote in a "talking points" memo sent to advisers and high-profile supporters. "It will set the race going forward and today, Jeb Bush is in a very strong position in the state."[4]

Here was the putative favorite, scion of the Bush dynasty, with a massive war chest behind him and he couldn't even get out of the starting block. Jeb's fall was swift and unforeseen; he never registered with GOP voters. In the first contest in Iowa, he was throughly rejected. During the primaries, he would parade around with his 75 page "plan" that no one was interested in hearing and would make the oddest statements such as Trump's dim view of illegal immigration does "not represent the values of the Republican party." If that's true, then those values are pro-amnesty. "Yes, they broke the law, but it's not a felony. It's an act of love, it's an act of commitment to your family," Bush said of illegal immigrants. He also made the bizarre pronouncement, but one that nonetheless crystallized his view of conservative Republican voters by stating that, You have to lose the primary, to win the General."

Jeb finished a disappointing fourth in New Hampshire and his campaign was now prepared to die on another hill: South Carolina. That state was going to be the Alamo for the Bush campaign. His strategists believed, in part because of his recent intemperate statements, that this would be the moment that Trump would finally come crashing back to earth. Instead, when all the votes were counted, actual Republican voters defied the entreaties from the establishment not to nominate a person who would be a sure loser against Clinton, but also defied the predictions of the by now clueless pundits.

In fact, not only did Trump vanquish Jeb, yet again, but also his astonishing victory was broad as it was deep. Trump didn't win across the board, but it was close. According to exit polls, he won men and women. He won voters who are evangelical Christians and those who are not. He won veterans and non-veterans. He cleaned up among the 46 percent of voters who do not have a college degree and nearly tied Marco Rubio, 25 percent to Rubio's 27 percent, among those who do. He won among voters who think terrorism is the top issue, and among voters who think the economy is the top issue, and among voters who think immigration is the top issue, and tied Rubio and Ted Cruz among voters who say government spending is the top issue.

In a very real sense, for Jeb Bush, the race was over the moment Trump announced. The posture of the two candidates couldn't have been more different. Trump had tapped into the incipient anger that the Bush loyalists completely missed. The voters wanted a candidate who could fight back and brawl. They wanted a candidate that would take on the left-wing bias of the Mainstream Media-Democratic Party-Complex that had never gone unchallenged by a Republican candidate. Jeb Bush, clearly wasn't the man for this job. He and his staff were locked into a sequestered political world where in their minds, not much had changed since the George W. Bush Administration. They were all asleep at the helm and Jeb's wish to have debates about policy fell upon deaf ears.

Republican primary voters weren't impressed with Jeb's massive war chest, nor were they impressed by the tiresome and insipid campaign message he was peddling. As was painfully obvious from the results of the early primary contests, the Republican primary electorate simply wasn't buying what Jeb's consultants were selling.

Jeb Suspends His Campaign

Declared the prohibitive favorite when he announced interest in running back in December, 2014, after a dreadful fourth place finish in South Carolina, Jeb Bush suspended his campaign ignominiously. As he acknowledged, the voters had indeed spoken and what was made abundantly clear, not only after his poor fourth place finish in South Carolina, but throughout the entire primary season, is that the Republican electorate were thoroughly rejecting the Establishment's policy priorities. Bush's final humiliation was the catalyst for the establishment to issue their desperate battle cry: "all hands on deck for Marco!' Bush's withdrawal from the race shattered the illusions of the establishment that Republican voters were compliant, malleable and content and forever willing to take one for the team.

After South Carolina, the attacks and foreboding about Trump increased in frequency and the vitriol leveled against the now undisputed front-runner was heightened. Here is what Senator Lindsey Graham had to say about his party's front runner, "I don't think he's a Republican, I don't think he's a conservative, I think his campaign's built on xenophobia, race-baiting and religious bigotry. I think he'd be a disaster for our party." Many pundits, consultants and other establishment politicians rallied to the cause. Others joined the lynch mob chorus claiming that Trump was an heretic guilty of desecrating and casting aside the ideals and true guiding principles of conservatism and in the process, was destroying the "Republican Brand."

Autopsy Report Backfires

Jeb's loss in South Carolina particularly jolted many members of the establishment. Many of the party's elites realized that when Bush's campaign died, so too did the Autopsy Report and any chance of using it as a guiding strategy for the party's nominee or for the future direction of the party. The implosion of Jeb Bush's campaign is instructive on another more fundamental level. The direction of the party favored by Bush Republicans as incorporated in the Autopsy Report was soundly rejected as being suicidal and wholly incompatible with the wishes and policy preferences of actual GOP voters.

What the Bush faithful who authored the Report failed to recognize was that the party, as constituted at the time of McCain's loss in 2012, was in its death throes. The Report was more an obituary than a blueprint for the future of the GOP. The voters would never again abide by the horribly misguided and backward-looking principles of Bush Republicanism. The fact that the report's authors were so stunned at the drubbing Jeb received in the primaries was indicative of a party that no longer understood, nor served the interests of its constituents.

Peter Spiliakos, writing in *National Review* analyzed this widening, and in the end irreconcilable gap between the preference of GOP elites and that of its voters, especially on the crucial issue of immigration. Spilakos addresses the underlying assumption of the Autopsy, namely that in order to win, the Republican Party needs be build a broad coalition and temper its conservatism. The elites believed that the party needed to be more open and "moderate." As Spilakos further notes, this argument is utterly specious, "There is just one problem: the alleged supporters of moderation and openness are actually extremists who are tearing their party apart in pursuit of unpopular policies.

Let's start with the supposed moderation. The Republican National Committee's autopsy is no moderate document. It has nothing to say of Mitt Romney's (and the Republican Party's) support for a politically toxic combination of high-earner tax reductions and entitlement cuts. It has nothing to say about learning from Bush's disastrous Iraq policy. The only alleged moderation and openness is in calling for "comprehensive immigration reform."

This is a Washington euphemism for a combination of upfront legalization of the existing population of unauthorized immigrants, plus expansion of future immigration."[1]

The madness inherent in the Autopsy Report is that it advocates policies that are unpopular. As Spilakos observes, "Unfortunately for the self-proclaimed Republican pragmatists, only 7 percent of Republicans, 17 percent of independents and 20 percent of Democrats favor increasing immigration."

As Spilakos further observes, what the rank and file voters of the party finally realized is that, The Republican establishment is populated with extremist, politically suicidal fanatics, but the Republican politicians can't see it because they don't measure moderation by public opinion. They measure moderation by the social status of the people holding the opinion. Republican officeholders, lobbyists, and consultants overwhelmingly hold one set of opinions on immigration (pro-amnesty, pro-increasing immigration, contemptuous of immigration enforcement.) That opinion is shared by the mass of the party's donors, and the business trade associations. It is shared by the mainstream media. That becomes the universe for Republican politicians. The vast majority of Americans who don't share those opinions only exists as a vague, despicable, fringe minority.[2]

The collapse of Marco Rubio

The Florida primary results must have been painful for Marco Rubio fans to watch. Convinced that he would be the last man standing, Trump visited upon the Senator from Florida a painful beating so bad that it was hard to see how Rubio could recover. It was clear that his strategy of taking on Trump one on one was a mistake, a bad tactical error which he openly acknowledged a week before the Florida votes were cast. The Marco hype was in essence, all about Marco. He was not a transcendent politician but merely an ambitious young politician in a hurry.

Commenting on Rubio's humbling defeat, Michael Brendan Dougherty observed that, Rubio has certainly been the beneficiary of media expectations that he would make the most formidable nominee. Every moment is a Rubio moment and South Carolina was no different. It is annoying to anyone who is not sold on him that Rubio seems to "win" according to the media's made-up spread even when he finished third in Iowa, fifth in New Hampshire, and a second that was a hair away from third in South Carolina. But the Rubio expectations game is based on national polls that show him being acceptable to the largest blocs of the party and competitive in the general election. Rubio wins among people who have college diplomas and Republicans who have high-paying jobs. He is acceptable to most of the party, but he is only truly beloved by the political class itself.[1]

The Gand of Eight betrayal

For those who had hoped that Rubio would thwart the Trump juggernaut, his supporters were in for a profound disappointment as their knight in shining armor fell prey to a Trump onslaught in Marco's home state of Florida. But, why would they have thought he could have prevailed? Catapulted into his Senate seat through the work of the Tea Party insurgents, Rubio began his betrayal shortly after his election. His involvement as cavorting Chuck Schumer's chump in another Comprehensive Immigration Reform boondoggle infuriated his supporters. They exacted their revenge with a vengeance in the primary.

The one issue that had earned Rubio the support of Florida Tea Party voters was his stance on immigration, After his election to the Senate, Rubio waffled and changed considerably on an issue that was pivotal for voters. At times, his positions as a Senator were diametrically opposed to his promises of no amnesty for illegal immigrants. The more he consorted with Schumer and McCain, the more his image suffered back home with his Tea Party supporters, who rightly felt that Rubio had stabbed them in the back. Rubio's flip flops on immigration were indicative of his primary weakness as a candidate: he was a man in a hurry with unbridled ambition and if he had to change his policy positions to get ahead, so be it.

It was obvious that Rubio wanted to court the establishment for an anticipated presidential run. It is important to note that in 2013 when the Comprehensive Immigration Reform bill went down in flames, Rubio, as well as most Republican politicians, could not see the brewing storm on the horizon. Rubio probably decided that his best chance for the nomination was to run through the establishment. Jeb had not expressed any interest in running at this time also. Rubio started to court the establishment donors. Marco, like many of his consultants, had badly read the mood of the electorate on the immigration question. Rubio's strategy was to follow the badly misguided Republican Party post mortem analysis of its 2012 presidential election defeat.

Rubio had stayed in the primary race far too long and had done damage to the prospects of the stop Trump crowd. Although he claimed there would be a reckoning for conservatives who support Trump, it is perhaps[1] he who will face a reckoning if he attempts elected office. As an indication of how little they had learned, after Rubio's defeat, many of his donors used the identical language that Democratic politicians and strategists have trumpeted for years: that today's Republican Party is a party of old white guys. Couldn't they come up with a more original line? This is yet another example of the establishment letting the Democratic Party, the media and liberals define the party's problems and the appropriate solutions.

Trump as a String of Primary Victories

When he finished second in the Iowa caucuses Monday, February 1, 2016, Trump narrowly lost the Iowa caucus to Ted Cruz, who received 27.6 percent of the votes counted in the caucus meetings, with Trump at 24.3 percent, and Rubio at 23.1 percent.

Ever since his strong second place finish in Iowa, the pundits had completely missed the rise of Trump, in fact, many had confidently predicted that he would simply burn out like a shooting star. The problem with the "expert" commentators and analysts is that they seemed incapable of learning from their spurious prior predictions about Trump. Trump dispatched all the establishment favorites in the primaries with alacrity, because he acted as a vehicle through which GOP voters could express their disapprobation with the status quo.

Trump was winning not only because of his die-hard supporters, who embraced his "Make America Great Again" theme, but also because he was bringing in a whole array of disaffected voters, who were disgusted with the status quo, especially those dinosaurs still running the Republican Party. As John O' Sullivan noted in *National Review*, "At first it seemed that Trump was addressing a relatively limited and cohesive group — a declining white working class. But as his rhetoric resounded and as voters responded to him in polls, it became clear that his appeal was to a much wider swath of American life. As my colleague Ramesh Ponnuru wrote after New Hampshire: "He also swept nearly every demographic category. He won young and old, men and women, independents and Republicans, first-time voters and returning ones, moderates and people who call themselves 'very conservative.' He carried every education group, albeit with a narrow margin among those with advanced college degrees."

The same effect was even stronger in the South Carolina results. There is clearly a larger pool of voters discontented with the mainstream parties and with the menu of policies and attitudes they offer than we realized before the election season woke us up.[1]

Establishment Panics

The view of establishment Republicans after Trump's resounding victory in New Hampshire was no different than that of pundits, pollsters and Republican consultants, it wasn't a question as to whether Trump was going to lose a general election contest against Hillary Clinton, but by how much. After the New Hampshire primary, Senate Majority Leader, Mitch McConnell laid out a plan to GOP leaders that would have lawmakers break with Mr. Trump in a general election[1]. After, Trump's victory in New Hampshire, leaders of the party began to panic. On February 19, 2016 party insiders and donors met in Washington. Karl Rove, a member of the Republican consultant class and Bush loyalist insisted that, despite his string of victories, it was not too late to derail Trump. The problem with Rove, was that his strategic advice was outdated; compassionate conservatism had been tried and rejected by the voters. Rove was old-school, pedaling the same tiresome electoral strategies embodied in the Autopsy Report and that GOP voters were rejecting. 2016 was not the year to recycle Rove's "compassionate conservatism" philosophy.

At a meeting the next morning, the frustration of the establishment Republicans was evident. The *New York Times* reported that Governor Paul R. LePage of Maine erupted in frustration over the state of the 2016 race, saying Mr. Trump's nomination would deeply wound the Republican Party. Mr. LePage urged the governors to draft an open letter to the people, disavowing Mr. Trump and his divisive brand of politics.[2]

However disconsolate party leaders may have been at the prospect of Trump as the nominee, no consensus emerged as to who would be the best candidate to stop him. John Kasich, a legend in his own mind, refused to stand down and unite behind another candidate, believing erroneously, that others would gravitate and consolidate behind him if he were to win his home state of Ohio. Thus efforts to unite warring candidates behind a single candidate failed.

The *New York Times* further observed that so convinced were leaders of the GOP that Trump would bring the party down with him in a general election contest, that according to senators at the February 20th luncheon, Mitch

McConnell began preparing senators for the prospect of a Trump nomination, assuring them that, if it threatened to harm them in the general election, they could run negative ads about Mr. Trump to create space between him and Republican senators seeking re-election. Mr. McConnell has raised the possibility of treating Mr. Trump's loss as a given and describing a Republican Senate to voters as a necessary check on a President Hillary Clinton.[3]

The prevailing wisdom still seemed to be that despite Trump's impressive victories against experienced party regulars, his campaign, at some point would run out of steam and if not, there was always the chance of heading him off at the pass by turning the convention into a contested nomination, this, despite the fact that GOP primary voters had overwhelmingly picked Trump as the candidate among the field that they wanted to be their standard bearer. Since it was no secret that Trump would be going up against the candidate who many had claimed was a shoo-in, did the Trump supporters know something that the leaders of the Republican party didn't? Some reasoned that since Rubio's fifth and Bush's fourth place finishes in New Hampshire, there was still hope that Bush could turn his ship around in South Carolina and then build on a solid victory to acquire momentum going forward. How Bush supporters thought a fourth place finish in New Hampshire would be a springboard for South Carolina was mystifying.

Although after South Carolina, it was evident the establishment was prepared to do anything to stop Trump, imagine what that would signal to longtime loyal conservative GOP voters. John O' Sullivan writing in *National Review* provides an insight into the ramifications of a GOP ticket with Rubio at the top, "The set-up most likely to produce that self-destructive result would be one that put Rubio at the top of the ticket. Rubio is the poster boy for the liberal immigration policies that Trump launched his campaign by opposing. He incarnates the theory that the U.S. economy can be be endlessly stimulated by importing cheap labor to hold down costs. So, as Mickey Kaus has pointed out, his nomination would be a sign to the voters, including the Trump people, that the GOP's brief flirtation with the idea of raising low incomes by tightening the labor market by reducing immigration had been defeated inside the party. Senator Jeff Sessions would be down, the donor class back, and the GOP's new converts out — or at least heavily discouraged."[4]

Romney Harshly Criticizes Trump

On March 3, 2016, Mitt Romney, who had once sought Trump's blessing when he was a candidate in 2012, excoriated the party's putative nominee.

In the hours before the GOP debate in Utah, Mitt Romney offered his own thorough, pragmatic denouncement of his party's presidential frontrunner in Salt Lake City, labeling Trump as a "phony" and a "fraud" who might destroy the GOP, and warning that his demagoguery is reminiscent of a "brand of anger that has led other nations into the abyss."

If any one had any questions about how Romney felt, he added,"Today, there is a contest between Trumpism and Republicanism. Through the calculated statements of its leader, Trumpism has become associated with racism, misogyny, bigotry, xenophobia, vulgarity and, most recently, threats and violence. I am repulsed by each and every one of these."

Though Romney's harsh comments may have warmed the hearts of the donor class and party leaders, the GOP rank and file had a completely different view of the establishment's assault on Trump. On the eve of the Michigan primary, Byron York of the *Washington Examiner* took the pulse of some of the GOP voters in the state. Many found Romney's comments to be over the top and inexplicable:

> "I personally didn't like it," said Rani Escamilla, of Sterling Heights. "He ran, I voted for him, now he's done, stay away, let's move on."
> "I think it's utterly disgraceful that the GOP is putting up everything they can to stop Trump," said Rani's friend Deanna Schwarz, of Wolverine Lake. "I think what [Romney] said was disgraceful, and I think it was the words of the GOP. It may not have been his words, because when he ran against Obama, he didn't talk that tough. So I don't think they were his words."[1]

As York reported, Republican voters of Michigan had quite a different view of Trump than that of the party: "there's no doubt he is connecting with many, many unhappy Republicans in Michigan. They feel their party has let them down, and is still letting them down by trying to sink Trump. Their way of fighting back is to cast a Trump vote on Tuesday."

And Then There Was One

After Trump's loss in Wisconsin, talk of a contested convention continued unabated amongst the chattering classes. Once Trump dispatched Cruz and Kasisch in Indiana, apprehension in the ranks of the establishment set in. Even though he had pledged to support the Republican nominee early on in the primary season, Bush was clearly peeved that his style of Republicanism was resoundingly rejected by voters. Unable to deal with the humiliating defeat, Jeb decided to take his toys and go home, declaring that he couldn't possibly support Trump because he was not a true "conservative."

One can only marvel at this spectacle of sore losers, particularly when it comes to Bush.

Then, there was the Speaker of the House, Paul Ryan, who could not bring himself to pledge support for the nominee of his party, elected by Republican primary voters— consistently. He expressed to Jake Tapper on CNN his displeasure with the party's presumptive nominee. Tapper obviously pressed him on the innate contradiction of a prominent leader of the party distancing himself from the putative front runner. This was music to the ears of the cable TV commentators and anchors. Ryan simply played publicly the role of the Republican dupe during the exchange. Who could have imagined such a spectacle, of intra-party bickering and internecine warfare before a presidential election? Some members of the never Trump crowd proclaimed they would be happy to see Hilary Clinton elected before they would support their own party's standard bearer.

The vituperation directed at Trump by his Republican party detractors was unprecedented. It is instructive to note the substantial difference between Democrats and Republicans in terms of the support for the nominee of their respective party. Despite being the subject of a pending criminal investigation, every Democratic politician exhibited unswerving loyalty for the presumed nominee of their party, Hillary Clinton.

Pat Buchanan noted that Trump had brought into the Republican fold new voters, "A new "New Majority" has been marching to the polls and voting Republican, a majority unlike any seen since the 49-state landslides of the Nixon and Reagan eras.

Buchanan responded to papers like the *Washington Post*, that characterized Trump's supporters as spiteful and racist,

"If this energy can be maintained, if those throngs of Republican voters can be united in the fall, then the party can hold Congress, capture the While House and reconstitute the Supreme Court.

Come the ides of March, the GOP is going to be in need of its uniter and its statesmen. But today, all Republicans should ask themselves:

Are these folks coming out in droves to vote Republican really the bigoted, hateful and authoritarian people of the Post's depiction?

Or is this not the same old Post that has poured bile on conservatives for generations now in a panic that America's destiny may be torn away from it and restored to its rightful owners?"[1]

Trump Attacks Hillary

For purposes of analyzing why Trump had such appeal to conservative voters, it is instructive to note that no other GOP nominee relentlessly attacked Hillary the way Trump did, especially about her devious email scheme and her playing the woman card. During April, 2016, Trump coined and began using in earnest, the devastating phrase "Crooked Hillary." It was a name that stuck and that he used repeatedly and effectively. In North Dakota, at a rally, he assailed "Crooked Hillary's" judgment and her fitness for the presidency. Similarly, at a rally in Indiana on May 2, 2016, Trump had harsh words for Hillary again, "If we win Indiana, it's over, okay? It's over. Then we can focus on Crooked Hillary. Please, let's focus on Crooked Hillary. We're going to make America great again. I love you. Get out there and vote on Tuesday."[1]

Even though "Crooked Hillary" was an accurate description, based on the extent and breath of her corruption, no other Republican candidate or Republican Party official would have dared utter those words, before, during or after the campaign, for fear of being reprimanded by the campaign police in the Mainstream Media-Democratic Party-Complex. Trump demonstrated by his caustic rhetoric, that he was not going to be bound by any such limitations.

During the campaign, Hillary thought it wise to dig into the Democratic Party's bag of tricks and employ the tried and true "war against women" stratagem that they used, with the able assistance of their allies in the media, against dimwitted and compliant old School Republicans. Trump was the first nominee who refused to be cowed by such nonsense. Indeed, when it came to the war against women Sword of Damocles, Trump again, was the first Republican to realize that the debauchery of his opponent's husband, provided him with more than enough rope to put a noose around Hillary's neck.

PART TWO

THE DEMOCRATS

CHAPTER SEVEN
The Party

One of the most memorable photographs to emerge from John F. Kennedy's 1960 Presidential campaign was that of him, completely at ease, smiling while shaking the hand of a beaming soot-covered one-armed coal miner in West Virginia. One can surmise that miner's exuberance in the presence of the wealthy Bostonian was based on the knowledge that he and his fellow miners knew, that Kennedy, as a Democrat, had an affinity and admiration for them — an affection, which they reciprocated heartily. In terms of assessing by comparison, the soul of the modern day Democratic Party in 2016, can anyone imagine Hillary Clinton mingling with common folk in the same manner as the beloved JFK?

Since the end of the Carter Administration, the Democratic Party has slowly evolved from the party of the "working man" into an institution that speaks exclusively to a coalition of minorities clustered in urban areas, those in academia, wealthy elites and gentry liberals A glimpse of a blue/red colored map by county reveals a party whose support is predominately bi-coastal; its reach in the great heartland eradicated. Today's Democratic Party welcomes as one of its new constituencies captains of the social media sectors, whose knowledge-based companies produce no tangible goods. Indeed, some of the party's most affluent donors revile the manufacturing sector and its ancillary businesses, as they believe it contributes to the warming of the planet. As such, they have no compunction about putting people in the nations vast energy sector out of work if it will assuage their concerns about climate change. The Democrats posture towards those who will lose their jobs? Let them eat cake.

Despite these fundamental changes in the composition of the party's leaders, donors and core constituencies, Democrats, with the willing and able assistance of the broadcast networks, have been masterful in perpetuating the myth that they exclusively have an indelible bond with the "common man" and the working classes.

This self-indulgent and obsolete narrative in conjunction with the belief that they are immune from criticism, helps explain why, leaders of the "party of the people" had no qualms in nominating as its standard-bearer, the fabulously wealthy and privileged John Kerry. Because of their enormous self-regard, premised on the belief in their intellectual and moral superiority, is so firmly embedded in the consciousness of the Democratic Party, neither the party nor the media could appreciate the irony of nominating a multi-millionaire, who docks his yacht in Rhode Island to evade Massachusetts' excise tax, as the exemplar of the party of the poor and dispossessed.

Hillary's 2016 quest for the White House provided yet another example of the party and the media's divorce from reality. The Clinton's sordid acquisition of wealth knew no bounds. They engaged in this self- aggrandizement shamelessly, with a wanton disregard for decorum, restraint or any sense of propriety. The duplicity and chicanery attendant in their naked pursuit of riches was well known to the party. Yet, did the Democrats or the media, who were content to ignore these brazen and grotesque violations of the public trust, ever in a rare moment of introspection, suspect that the disgraceful conduct of the Clintons and their overweening sense of entitlement might be viewed with a jaundiced eye in middle America or by the "common man," on whose behalf the Democrats purportedly toil?

This striking metamorphosis of the party is further evidenced by the fact that not one of its leaders believed for a moment that it might be problematic to offer as the voice of the party of the indigent and struggling working classes, a woman who had grown filthy rich giving banal thirty-minute speeches to Wall Street banks for an astronomical sum of $250,000 and who was in the midst of battling the scandal of her families slush fund, the Clinton Foundation, through which she and her husband leveraged their years of "public service" into a $200 million lucre. If they accomplished little else, it can be said that Hillary and Bill are solely responsible for exploding the long-held caricature of Republicans as the party of the rich.

Despite trotting out its wealthy and comfortably detached Hollywood cohorts and stars of the entertainment industry to bolster Hillary's cause, the party nonetheless believed that it could still rely on the fable of its role as the vanguard of the working class. The election of 2016 challenged the underpinnings of this narrative as never before. By its words and deeds, the Clinton campaign represented the culmination of the festering and incipient contradictions within the Democratic Party, exposing the ever widening gulf between the perception of the party as the natural ally and protector of the "common man" and the stark reality of the public deportment of its appointed, or in the case of Hillary, its anointed leaders. During the campaign, these fissures started to surface, over time they became more pronounced and in the end, finally cracked.

One of the most serious political miscalculations the Democrats made in 2016 was their belief that the country had stood still during the eight years of the Obama presidency. While party leaders may have taken comfort in the fact that Obama enjoyed above-average favorability ratings, it couldn't mask the fact that while Obama was eminently likable and personally popular with most of the electorate, his policies were not. The party of identity politics was basking in adulation at having the nation's first African-American president and many party leaders were completely oblivious to the damage that Obama had done to the party at the state level. During the eight years of his presidency, Democrats approached extinction levels in many state houses. For those who had been paying attention, there was the stark realization that when Obama left the White House, the Democratic Party had only 16 governors left and faced 32 state legislatures fully under GOP control.

In 2014, Michael Barone, one of the authors of the *Almanac of American Politics*, in a prescient article asked the question, "Why has the Democratic Party fared so poorly under Obama's leadership? I can see two reasons: one ideological, one demographic.

Start with demographics. The Obama coalition, even more than Bill Clinton's, is based on overwhelming support from constituencies with some conflicting interests. It's a top-and-bottom coalition: he carried the very lowest and highest income and education groups, while his support sagged among those in the middle.

His strongest groups are blacks and gentry liberals -- the same two groups he gathered together when he got to design his own state Senate district in 2002. Majorities of both groups still support him, but perhaps with diminished enthusiasm. Black crowds unexpectedly started walking out before he finished talking at recent events in Prince George's County, Maryland, and Milwaukee. Moreover, the geographic clustering of blacks and gentry liberals in central cities, sympathetic suburbs and university towns puts the Obama Democrats at a disadvantage in equal-population districts where Republican voters are spread more evenly around.[1]"

Barone concludes by noting that, "Yes, Hillary Clinton leads in polls for 2016. But her numbers have been sagging. And other Democrats poll worse against not-very-well-known Republican alternatives than I can remember any party's potential candidates polling in the last half-century."[2]

What Democrats failed to appreciate was that many of those who who didn't live in bicoastal urban clusters of progressive cosmopolitanism were not terrible enamored of the policies and posture of Obama's faculty-lounge liberalism and the suffocating scourge of political correctness that accompanied it. For these voters, Hillary promised more of the same to a country that was weary of the stifling and oppressive speech and conduct codes.

Under the aegis of Obama's liberalism, the political commissars of progressivism had politicized every aspect of American life. Million dollar NFL player Colin Kapernick refused to stand for the national anthem, because in his eyes it was symbolic of the unfair way the country treats people "of color." The corrosive rot of political correctness was seeping into a network that was supposed to be the nations premier sports channel. It was the worst of in-your-face liberalism and with Hillary in the White House, there was every expectation that it would continue.

CHAPTER EIGHT

The Candidate

If there is any one phrase that best describes the mindset of the Democratic Party during the 2016 election cycle, it would be blissful ignorance. For a while, Trump's frequent gaffes and outbursts on the campaign trail and the concomitant effect this behavior had on his poll numbers, protected the Democrats from the enormity of their stupidity. Hillary's 2008 campaign had demonstrated one indisputable fact, she reeked of inauthenticity. A horrible candidate, she was stiff, haughty and dismissive.

She told us long ago that she was named "Hillary"after the famed New Zealander, who in 1953, became the first to scale Mount Everest. Apparently, no one told her parents that Sir Edmund Hillary didn't scale that peak until after she was born. And, if one wishes, unwisely, to continue to suspend disbelief while her lips are moving, the Wellesley College and Yale Law School graduate insisted that she tried to join the Marines in 1975, but was turned down because she was a woman. She said the FBI was merely conducting a "security review" into her emails; FBI Director James Comey said it was not an inquiry but an investigation. She said she dodged sniper fire when she landed in Bosnia; later video revealed her strolling carefree on the tarmac.

The late *New York Times* columnist, William Safire diagnosed her as a "congenital liar." She lies when it suits her purposes; she lies when it is expedient; she lies about matters both big and small, trivial and substantive. She lies when she doesn't need to lie; she lies about her lies. These well known traits are indicative of a woman who has no core, no center, no moral compass and no sense of self. Like her ever changing hairdos, Hillary's persona fits the mood of the moment, her particular audience, or her self-interest and preferred political narrative.

One wonders if those who were "Ready for Hillary" viewed her 2007 migraine-inducing, grotesque impersonation "I don't feel no ways tired…" performance to an African-American audience while speaking at the 42nd anniversary of Bloody Sunday, on March 7, 1965, when 600 civil rights marchers were attacked by police. This was Hillary at her best: pandering when necessary, willing to say anything if it would be politically expedient — even if she made a fool of herself in the process. The woman has no shame.

Whitewater, her cattle futures windfall profits, the Rose Law Firm billing records that mysteriously were found in a closet in the White House, and her firing of the White House travel office employees. The unsavory aspect of the Clintons and their capacity for disreputable behavior were all well known to the party; in Hillary, they knew exactly what they were getting. Nonetheless, to a party interested in nominating the first woman above all else, none of her well known and glaring flaws mattered. Her gender and historic candidacy obscured all her sins. And therein, lay the fatal miscalculation of the Democratic Party: they believed the rest of the country, or at least, most women would, like the party, overlook or ignore the overwhelming evidence that demonstrated that not only did Hillary have a nauseating overweening sense of entitlement, but also, that she was corrupt to the core.

The Democratic Party had ample notice of the Clinton's sordid past — both in Arkansas and in Washington. Scandal followed the Clintons wherever they went. Why party officials thought it would be a good ida to nominate the wife of a man who had previously defiled the office and subsequently was impeached will be an intriguing topic for historians to ponder.

Identity politics had a firm grip on the consciousness of the party so much so that it made a dispassionate assessment of her chances in an electoral contest impossible. Every single statement this woman had said in public about her private email server was a lie, only to be amended by another subsequent lie. There were warning signs galore that presented the party numerous opportunities to head off what surely they must have known would be an unmitigated disaster.

What, one wonders, was the party thinking after the State Department's scathing Inspector General's report? At that point, there was still time to right the ship, for it was taking on water. Trump at this point had closed the gap and news of her chicanery at the State Department continued to trickle out. The party's nominee was the subject of a pending criminal investigation — an unprecedented situation in American political history.

Even though Obama would instruct Comey to drop the matter, did the party truly believe that Hillary calling the criminal probe a little old "security review" or that it was the server and not her that was the subject of the FBI's inquiry, would put the matter to rest? More importantly, did the party seriously think or assume that most American would not miss the obvious and brazen falsehoods?

And, who in the party thought it would be a good idea to give both Clintons another lease on the White house *carte blanche*? Bill had demonstrated once again during the campaign, his predilection for impropriety when he covertly met with Loretta Lynch. What did party officials think Bill Clinton was not capable of doing once he resided in the White House again? They apparently thought that it would be good idea to send back to 1600 Pennsylvania Avenue , a man who had previously tainted the office by having sex with a 22 year old intern. What reasonable person in command of his faculties could not foresee impending disaster? The failure to intervene tells us a great deal about the moral bankruptcy of the Democratic Party.

There can be only one explanation as to why the party thought that Hillary's baggage was of no consequence. They must have believed that Hillary would be immune from any fallout over her unscrupulous email scheme because the average voter would be either too stupid to understand and hence malleable enough to be receptive to Hillary's numerous lies, or they wouldn't care.

For the Democratic Party, March 2, 2015 would prove to be a watershed moment in the presidential sweepstakes of 2016. The *New York Times* broke the story about the existence of Hillary's private email server, established to avoid public and congressional scrutiny while she was Secretary of State. The revelation was shocking and later WikiLeaks e-mail disclosures would reveal that having no knowledge of Hillary's duplicity, her senior staff were caught completely off-guard.

For those in the party with their heads screwed on straight, there was no denying the fact that after March 2, 2015, Hillary was damaged goods, an unexploded bomb waiting to go off at any moment during the campaign. The party had ample warnings and numerous opportunities to staunch the bleeding and take steps to mitigate the risk of unforeseen revelations, but the disciples of identity politics and the feminists would have none of it. The truth of the matter was that for the Democratic Party, the die was cast. Live by the identity politics sword, die by the identity politics sword. *It was her turn.* Long before her official announcement, long before the first Democratic primary, those were the operative and determinative words.

How ironic and telling that Hillary's most ardent competitor proved to be a 70 year old Socialist who honeymooned in the Soviet Union and was not even a member of the party that was eager to accelerate her coronation. Bernie Sanders would prove to be a thorn in Hillary's side during the early stages of the primary battles. Despite being a long-shot, Sanders' unexpected string of primary victories proved embarrassing to the presumed front runner and ultimately would tarnish Hillary's star.

CHAPTER NINE
Early Revelations About Email

On March 2, 2015, the engine in Hillary's Scooby Doo van blew a gasket. On that day, the *New York Times* revealed for the first time that Hillary had conducted official government business as Secretary of State on a clandestine, private, and unauthorized email server that she exclusively controlled, and maintained in the basement of her Chapaqua residence.

Perhaps the most defining moment of her candidacy, would prove to be her disastrous U.N. Press conference held on March 15th, before she had even announced her official candidacy. From that moment forward, her bald face lies, prevarications and parsing that were an indelible and well known characteristic of both Clintons, would stain and seriously hamper her candidacy.

This would prove to be a significant event for the campaign because going forward, the email issue would plague her. Her insularity and colossal poor judgment prevented her from appreciating the catastrophic consequences of her actions. Her sense of entitlement was consistent with her belief that she could conduct official business of the United States Government through use of a private server over which she exercised complete control.

Ever since the Whitewater scandal of Bill's presidency in 1998, both Clintons felt that any political threat could be managed by appropriate media massaging, part of which entailed dispatching surrogates to attack those making the accusations. As Jonathan Allen and Amie Parnes, authors of *Shattered: Inside Hillary Clinton's Doomed Campaign* noted, "When news of her private e-mail server fist surfaced in the *New York Times* on March 2, 2015, she looked at it as the campaign's first wave of "choppy waters" rather than the tsunami that it would become."[1]

In an attempt to defend her indefensible actions, Hillary claimed that her predecessors, like Colin Powell had used similar systems. This feeble justification for her reckless and unprecedented actions was as disingenuous as it was patently false. Powell and others, at most, sent a small number of emails through private email accounts. They did not use a private server, under their sole custody and control, separate and distinct from official government systems, for 100 percent of their communications in their official capacity as the nation's chief diplomat.

By deliberately using a private email system exclusively for all of her official business as Secretary of State, Hillary was circumventing the Public Records Act as well as shielding her actions from Congressional oversight.

For several months after the email story became public, Hillary dismissed the growing public relations headwinds as much ado about nothing. She refused to issue an act of contrition, as she truly believed, as Secretary of State that she was entitled to establish her email communication in a manner she saw fit and hence, she had done nothing wrong.[2] Or, as she was so fond of exclaiming: "It was not in any way disallowed." Later WikiLeaks revelations put the lie to not only Hillary's seeming indifference over her reckless and unlawful conduct but to that of her most strident surrogates as well.

In this regard, compare Hillary's cavalier and arrogant attitude after the *New York Times* report with the reaction of some of her senior aides upon learning for the first time of the existence of her private email system. Many were stupefied. One close ally, Center for American Progress leader Neera Tanden, was still fuming months after the March 2d disclosure of Hillary's private communications system. In one email, Tanden pressed Campaign Chairman John Podesta on who gave Clinton permission to use the system:

"Do we actually know who told Hillary she could use a private email? And has that person been drawn and quartered?" Tanden wrote in July. "Like whole thing is f—ing insane." Other emails reveal that with the exception of a few

Hillary insiders, most of her aides weren't aware of the private arrangement.

On March 2, Podesta wrote to current Campaign Manager Robby Mook asking if Mook had "any idea of the depth of this story?" "Nope. We brought up the existence of emails in research this summer but were told that everything was taken care of," Mook wrote back at 1:32 a.m. on March 3. Podesta also wrote to Tanden airing his concerns on March 2, the day the story about Clinton's private email account broke. "Speaking of transparency, our friends [attorney David] Kendall, Cheryl and Phillipe [Reines] sure weren't forthcoming on the facts here," Podesta wrote. Tanden replied, implying that keeping the email setup a secret was likely Mills' doing. "This is a Cheryl special," Tanden wrote. "Know you love her, but this stuff is like her Achilles heel. Or kryptonite. She just can't say no to this s—. Why didn't they get this stuff out like 18 months ago? So crazy." Tanden added: "I guess I know the answer they wanted to get away with it."[3]

For many voters, Hillary's imperious, and dismissive attitude concerning her unique and unprecedented arrangement was more evidence that the Clintons for years had conducted themselves with the belief that they were not bound by the rules everyone else had had to follow. Hillary's exculpatory statements offered in support of her unconscionable conduct as well as her lack of remorse were some of the reasons her favorability ratings plummeted after news of her private server surfaced.

The Democratic Party and the Clinton's had a long and mutually beneficial, if at times tempestuous, relationship. The Clinton's predilection for shifty, knavish behavior was well know not only to members of the party, but to the American people as well. As soon as news of the emails broke, Hillary went into the familiar Clinton strategy of dissembling and outright denial and using the oft-repeated phrase, that her conduct was not "illegal" or not "disallowed", to justify her scandalous behavior. From the moment the news was made public, Hillary's comments and explanations for the highly unorthodox arrangement evolved constantly and were subject to further amendment and revision when her earlier statements were demonstrably proven to be false.

The party elders were on notice at this moment in time that they could expect that which they had witnessed countless times before with this couple: conduct, that at best was improper and inappropriate and at worst, felonious. Despite these early warning signs, the Democratic Party still remained loyal and committed to the identity politics justification for Hillary as the standard bearer for the party — all the evidence of her shocking behavior notwithstanding. The momentum for her candidacy was simply too strong to thwart, a decision, the party would later regret.

As Allen and Parnes note, "The president of the United States, and all the Democratic officials below him, were now embroiled in the end of scandal that reminded them of exactly what they didn't like about the Clintons: the secrecy and the willingness to jeopardize everyone else's interests in service of their own."[4] Hillary wouldn't launch her campaign for more than a month, and already she was neck-deep in a scandal that would overshadow almost everything she said and did for the next twenty months[5].

CHAPTER TEN
U.N. Press conference

Unable to contain the growing public outcry over her infamy, Hillary was forced to address her email issue at a press conference at the United Nations on March 10, 2015. While she admitted that she exclusively used a private, non-government email server while Secretary of State, her performance during the press conference was dreadful. Petulant from the start, she was haughty, arrogant, and unrepentant. And, to add insult to injury, she proclaimed with breathtaking audacity that "her" private server (yes, the one she used to conduct official government business) would remain *private*. She spoke in practiced Clintonian legalese: she, "fully complied with every rule I was governed under"

The woefully inadequate answers Clinton provided in terms of why she went to the trouble of setting up a private server in the first place would all be thoroughly discredited in the weeks subsequent to the U.N. press conference. Not only were her original statements brazen lies, it was discovered that she had deleted some 33,000 emails because she claimed they were personal and not work-related. Who made the determination as to which emails were "personal"? Hillary and Hillary alone. Clinton dispatched her long-time confidante Cheryl Mills to conduct the search and then aid in the determination of which emails would be deleted.

A subsequent FBI report made it clear that the procedure employed by Mills was suspicious and that there was evidence of massive document destruction and clear intent to withhold material evidence.[1] Clinton's claim that the "personal" nature of the emails deleted pertained to matters such as her yoga classes or plans related to her daughter Chelsea's wedding. It was discovered that one of the reasons for creating the private system was to keep prying eyes away from those emails that showed the favors that Hillary was dispensing and/or promises she made for access while she was Secretary of State to those who made "donations" to the Clinton Foundation. Some of the promises for favors or special meetings with Clinton in her role of Secretary of State were made in the form of outlandish speaking fees to Bill Clinton while she was acting as the nation's chief diplomat.

Shortly after the *New York Times* story, the private server was wiped clean with a software program called "Bleach Bit." In the lexicon of criminal law this is known as "consciousness of guilt."

CHAPTER ELEVEN
Hillary Adresses Email Issue

Hillary and some of her most trusted aides completely misread and were inexplicably blind to the mortal danger the e-mail story posed to her candidacy. The failure to react swiftly to the bad news demonstrates how the Clinton campaign was staffed with sycophants, toadies and those who had their eyes on a lofty position in the upcoming Clinton Administration. Challenging the wisdom of Hillary's decisions was not in their job descriptions. Since most of her staff believed that nothing was going to get in the way of their boss's historic and inevitable coronation, their judgment was hopelessly compromised: "At first, her aides tried to laugh it off. The day after the story popped online, Palmieri and Schwerin floated the idea of inserting a joke about the e-mails into an upcoming speech to the abortion rights group EMILY's List. It was neither the first nor the last time that her team's instincts ran toward making light of the situation."[1]

Even though the issue was killing her politically, for months from the moment the story broke, Hillary steadfastly refused to admit she did anything wrong and she stubbornly refused to atone or apologize. In fact, on one of those rare occasions when she deigned to answer questions from the press, she was asked whether she had wiped her server clean. She responded flippantly, "What, like with a cloth or something?" Hillary was a battle-hardened veteran of numerous political scandals that the Clinton's always seemed to survive. She must have thought to herself that this was just another blip on her way to the presidency and could be dealt with in the same manner as Whitewater, Monica Lewinsky and the White House travel office: use her surrogates to contend nothing was amiss; other Secretary's of States had done the same thing; her actions were not criminal, so she should be exonerated; and, a Clinton favorite: "it's old news."

Even though Hillary believed the furor building over the email story was nothing more than an attempt by Republicans and her other detractors to derail her candidacy, her aides were beginning to get concerned. When she announced her candidacy in April, 2015, she had a 69 percent to 5 percent lead over Bernie Sanders. A poll taken in September 4th through September 8th saw her lead shrink dramatically to 37 percent to Sanders 27 percent. The Hillary campaign was cratering. As Howard Kurtz noted in mid October, 2015, "It's hard to score points when you're constantly seen as responding to investigators or rivals or media detractors. And the private server represents the classic self-inflicted wound."[2]

Finally, on September 8, 2015 during an interview with ABC's David Muir, "Hillary gave her team, the Democratic Party, and the press what they desperately wanted —full contrition for the decision she'd made in the first place. That having done so at the beginning might have saver her five months of political free fall didn't seem to register."[3] She told Muir that , I should've used two accounts. That was a mistake, I'm sorry about that. I take responsibility." But that feigned act of remorse by Hillary would not be the last the campaign would hear about the e-mail scandal.

CHAPTER TWELVE

Press Corps: Hillary's Cheerleaders

One of the reasons that Trump's victory against all odds was so significant is due to the fact that his opponent wasn't just Hillary Clinton, it was the entire mainstream media, who from the start, were in Hillary's corner. In terms of her many advantages at the start of the general election, this perhaps was the most significant, most notably in light of her burgeoning email scandal and the media's willingness to protect her from the adverse ramifications of these bombshell revelations.

At first the love affair was expressed by a blithe indifference to cover stories that would be harmful to the Clinton campaign or by intentionally mischaracterizing her scandals as nothing more than the rumblings of the vast right wing conspiracy. Later, when Donald Trump, whom the press treated as a novelty item or an entertaining circus clown, began to threaten Hillary's ascension to the White House, the policy of a virtual blackout on negative Hillary stories gave way to outright advocacy for the media's candidate of choice. The more Trump advanced on the inevitable candidate, the more overt the bias against him became. All pretenses of objectivity were jettisoned in order to respond to the clarion call of "All hands on deck", when the Clinton campaign began to crater.

In order to appreciate how craven the press corps acted, the Scooby Doo van was treated as the 21st century equivalent of the royal carriage. Reporters would all on cue chase down the vehicle and when Her Majesty emerged, they would hang on to her every word, which due to her ongoing scandals, were sparse. Hillary peremptorily dismissed them, her lips sealed and they welcomed the abuse. Hillary treated her courtiers with appropriate disdain because she knew she was immune from any real probing questions or criticism because those who purportedly are supposed to speak truth to power, in the end, were all rooting for the home team.

Here is an example, as collected by Larry O' Connor, of some of the questions our intrepid reporters asked the woman who would be president after a 280 day absence with the press:

"You're on the cusp of being the first female nominee of a major party. What does that mean to you and how are you reflecting on that?"

"No matter what happens tomorrow, Bernie Sanders says the convention in Philadelphia will be contested. Do you think there is anything you can do to change that at this point?"

"Is it setting in that you might be making serious history tomorrow?"

"Some prominent Democrats have come out saying 'we maybe need to reevaluate the super delegate system more broadly. irrespective of what happens in this primary, do you support looking into that and, perhaps, getting rid of that?"

"Do you think Sen. Sanders will concede as you did in 2008?"

"What role would you like the president to play in your campaign?"

"Last night when you took stage in Sacramento, there was a woman standing next to me who was absolutely sobbing. And she said, you know, 'it's time, it's past time.' And you see the women, you see people here. People just come up to you and, {gasp} they get tears in their eyes. Do you feel… do you feel the weight of what this means to people?"

"Do you expect the president's endorsement some time this week?"[1]

Not one question about the criminal email investigation nor any inquiry about the pay-to-play influence peddling that occurred in the Clinton Foundation.

WikiLeaks hacked emails would later reveal how giddy the Clinton campaign was that the media was all aboard the "Ready for Hillary" train. In one email, her staff bragged, "every single interviewer was for her" during a visit to Michigan during the Democratic primary season. Notes by Nick Merrill, Clinton's traveling press secretary indicate a cozy relationship with the press. In one email, Merrill recounts dealings with members of the Fourth Estate: "[Six] radio interviews and [two] coffee shops this morning," Merrill wrote. "Flint came up in every one, and then education, and [Affordable Care Act] ACA," he said. "No flags. Every single interviewer was for her."[2]

If left to the mainstream media, the story of Hillary's private server might never have been reported. As *Investors Business Daily*, reported, "Normally, with a scandal this juicy and involving a would-be president, reporters would be falling over themselves to "advance the story." But "normal" never seems to apply when a scandal involves a Democrat. The FBI has 147 investigators focused on the Clinton email case. One wonders how many investigative reporters the New York Times, the Post, and all the other big media outlets have."[3]

CHAPTER THIRTEEN

Beginnings of the race

Even though she was the presumed front runner, two months after her official announcement, Hillary's fortunes began to decline precipitously. By July, 2015, her campaign was taking on water and her approval ratings had fallen below 40 percent. Given the substantial advantages she had over all the other "candidates" in the race, her diminished standing was ominous. In terms of gauging how far she had fallen, when she announced in April, 2015, she led Sanders 69% to 5%; by late September, 2015 it was 37% to 27%. It was clear to everyone but a clueless Hillary that disclosures about her email practices had an adverse impact on her standing in the race.

In both word and deed, Hillary felt that she was entitled to the presidency, yet she exhibited an insouciance about to the public's perception of her persona as well as the reality of her numerous s improprieties.

By September, 2015, due to her total lack of remorse for her unprecedented and surreptitious use of a private server had convinced most Americans that Hillary was a liar who couldn't be trusted.

Her approval ratings during her tenure as Secretary of State were fairly good. As soon as she announced her candidacy in April, revelations concerning her emails started to drip out slowly. Next came numerous questions about the sordid practice of doling out favors to donors to the Clinton Foundation. Then there were the questions about her astronomical speaking fees to Wall Street banks. As if to demonstrate her political tone-deafness, when asked about the money she received, her response was, "that's what they paid me." As if this impudent response was sufficient to dispense with any further inquiries about the propriety surrounding the matter. Hillary would learn later that her most tenacious opponent had no intention of letting the matter rest.

From the beginning of her quest for the White House, one of the most exasperating tasks for Clinton's campaign staff was creating a slogan that would succinctly and clearly spell out how a Hillary presidency would favorably impact voters lives. From the start, Clinton believed it was the responsibility of her staff to create a winning brand and message that would captivate, resonate and inspire voters. Oddly, and in the end, quite tellingly, Clinton herself had never settled, nor felt the need to craft, a compelling message to voters as to why they should elect her president.

One of the reasons she could never present to voters a persuasive justification for her candidacy is that Hillary always viewed her quest for the presidency as an entitlement. She didn't need the approval of voters, as the campaign was merely a necessary evil, a formality towards fulfilling her destiny to the throne. And, this was the view of many journalists as well, as Hillary undoubtedly knew.

Time and again, the campaign slogans kept changing. "Ready for Hillary"; "I'm with Her"; then, after Sanders pummeled her in New Hampshire, "Breaking Barriers." At some point in the campaign, the "Stronger Together" slogan was rolled out. Despite the modifications, one attribute remained the same: the message in the end was all about her and the campaign could never surmount this debilitating limitation. By the time she began to square off with Trump, Hillary still could not offer voters a coherent idea or perception of how a Clinton II Administration would improve their lives.

The difficulty of finding and presenting an appropriate message that was captivating was a problem that was evident from the start. As Allen and Parnes recall, "Some of her speechwriters who worked on her announcement speech she gave at her kickoff rally on Roosevelt Island would recall later that the speech failed to connect Hilary to a cause larger than herself. She offered no rationalization for her candidacy other than she would be the first woman president. There was never any question, and no adviser prompted discussion of 'Why you, why now."[1]

Roger Stone explains that some of her advisers questioned the significance that Hillary placed on her gender throughout the campaign. A WikiLeaks disclosed email exchange dated March 22, 2014, between Hillary's campaign manager Robby Mook and her adviser/ attorney Cheryl Mills, copied to John Podesta, indicated clearly all three had their doubts from the start about the likely success of a gender-based campaign focused on the premise that Hillary would be the first woman president,

> "In fact, I think running on her gender would be the same mistake as 2008, i.e., having a message at odds with what voters ultimately want," Mook said. "She ran on experience when voters wanted change … and sure there was plenty of data in polls with voters saying her experience appealed to them. But that was missing the larger point — voters wanted change." Mook felt it was similar in 2016. "Same deal here — lots of people are going to say it would be neat for a woman to be president but that doesn't mean that's actually why they will vote for her. That's likely to be how she will handle the economy and relate to the middle class. It's also risky because injecting gender makes her candidacy about her and not the voters and making their lives better." Podesta agreed. "One caveat," he said simply, "gender will be a big field and volunteer motivator, but won't close the deal."[2]

The goal of nominating the first woman president, while significant for Hillary's feminist supporters, did not move or inspire millennials or many other professional women who were not jumping on the gender identity politics bandwagon. This disturbing and foretelling trend had been evident during the primaries. As the *New York Times* reported, "Women were expected to help power Mrs. Clinton to the Democratic nomination, but as she struggles to overcome a tough challenge from Mr. Sanders and trails him in New Hampshire polls, her support among them has been surprisingly shaky. Young women, in particular, have been drawn to the septuagenarian socialist from Vermont, and the dynamic has disappointed feminists who dreamed of Mrs. Clinton's election as a capstone to their long struggle for equality."

Desperate to avoid embarrassment, the cavalry was called in by the Clinton campaign to staunch the bleeding by reeducating these wayward women who apparently had not received the memo instructing them that their gender mandated a vote for the likely First. Woman. President. Hillary brought in former Secretary of State, Madeline Albright, who admonished those women who had strayed from the path to get with the elect Hillary program. At the rally, Albright, "talked about the importance of electing a woman to the country's highest office. In a dig at the "revolution" that Mr. Sanders, 74, often speaks of, she said the first female commander in chief would be a true revolution. And she scolded any woman who felt otherwise." Albright further added, "We can tell our story of how we climbed the ladder, and a lot of you younger women think it's done," Ms. Albright said of the broader fight for women's equality. "It's not done. There's a special place in hell for women who don't help each other!"

CHAPTER FOURTEEN

Sanders as An alternative

For a woman who was the presumptive favorite, with a massive war chest at her disposal and an army of advisors, Hillary's campaign had a perilous start, that should have sent up warning flags to her strategists. Sanders was catching fire: when Hillary had announced in April, 2015, she led Sanders 69 percent to 5 percent. According to one poll in September, 2015, Sanders was even with Hillary, 41 to 40 percent. On February 2, 2016, Clinton barely managed to squeak by the Socialist Senator from Vermont in the Iowa caucuses. The Iowa Democratic Party called the results the closest in its caucus history. One of the reasons, noted by Allen and Parnes, for Hillary's razor thin victory was that, "as Iowans took their last measure of the two candidates, what stood out was Bernie's energy and Hillary's dishonesty."[1] It is interesting to note that three months before the Iowa caucus, Sanders had trailed Hillary by 30 points. Sanders repeatedly brought up the astronomical speaking fees to Wall Street firms including one to Goldman Sachs where she netted $675,000 for her remarks.[2] This was not a good omen for the campaign heading into New Hampshire, where Sanders had been besting Hillary in the polls since September, 2015. By February, 2016 some polls had him beating Hillary by 20 points.

When Sanders began catching up to Hillary in Iowa in the fall, he also started to surge in New Hampshire. By this time, Sanders's favorability rating was in the nineties; Hillary's were in the low eighties. As the New Hampshire primary approached, Sanders was clobbering Hillary. Bill Clinton was astute enough to realize the problem. It was the inability to communicate to voters an inspiring message with which they could relate. "Bill may have thought he or Hillary could persuade voters. But she would have needed a stronger vision to make the case. She had plans for every imaginable corner of public policy, but they were loosely strung together. There was no simple vision unifying theme — no central, defining promise of a Hillary presidency.[3]"

As the authors of *Shattered: Inside Hillary Clinton's Doomed Campaign* observed, "After having campaigned in New Hampshire throughout January, Bill knew just as well as Hillary did that she was going to lose the sate. But he believed there was a change to keep the margin under ten points. Which would provide a moral victory. Meanwhile, the numbers were moving in the opposite direction."[4]

Allen and Parnes note further that Hillary's campaign message was constantly in a state of evolution, "In late January, as Hillary's campaign began to think about "evolving the core message," Ron Klain chimed in with a succinct analysis of what was missing. "We need to invest more time in describing what HRC wants to do for America, if she becomes President," he wrote to her top campaign brass. "What is it that she wants to do as President? How would America be different? What should people be excited about?…What we need to deliver is a more compelling message on America under HRC.[5]"

However, from the start, Hillary wanted no responsibility in crafting a message. "It was a vision Hillary herself couldn't articulate for them. But the one aspect of her campaign that she was most confident about was that none of the tribes, separately or in collaboration, had any idea how to construct a winning message for her. In her view, it was up to the people she paid to find the right message for her — a construction deeply at odds with the way Sanders and Trump built their campaigns around their own gut feelings about where to lead the country.[6] Hillary's inability or unwillingness to create by herself, a compelling message for her candidacy, was one of the reasons her quest for the White House was doomed. Allen and Parnes recall how Hillary's message was constantly in a process of evolution,

Hillary's New Hampshire concession speech would incorporate yet another new slogan: "Breaking Barriers." Her campaign gurus thought that this would show that she was the candidate for voters of color and of women, while Sanders was not.[7] "But for nearly a year on the campaign trail, she hadn't been able to connect all the dots. She spoke about "I" and "you" but almost never "we." When supporters declared their allegiance to her online, they did it with #I'm With Her. For whatever reason —she chalked it up to midwest modesty — she felt uncomfortable presenting herself as the heroine. And yet critics saw her reluctance to use "we" — like Bernie Sanders and Donald Trump and so many other candidates did — as evidence that her campaign was all about her."[8]

During the later stages of the primary contest, even after Hillary's impressive Super Tuesday wins, her loss in Michigan later was humiliating. It robbed her of a chance to put down Sanders for good. Hillary was furious with her staff and felt that they had let her down; they should have crafted a better strategy, even though she was the one who approved of the Michigan strategy. Allen and Parnes recall Hillary's sentiments,

It was hard enough to run agains Bernie Sanders, Donald Trump, the Republican National Committee, and the national media — plus slippery-lipped Joe Biden on any given day — without her own team screwing things up. The one person with whom she didn't seem particularly upset: herself. No one who drew a salary from the campaign would tell her that. It was a self-signed death warrant to raise a question about Hillary's competence — to he or anyone else — in loyalty-obsessed Clintonworld. Most of the people around her were jockeying to get closer to her, not to make her wonder about heir commitment. And many didn't know her very well personally. Even Huma Abedin, who was close to her, had all but given up on guiding her toward shifting course. She had long since started telling Hillary allies outside the campaign to take their complaints and suffusions straight to the candidate. For the mercenaries who had joined the campaign in hopes of finding jobs in the next administration, there was little percentage in getting on Hillary's bad side.[9]

Hillary's bewildered response to the Michigan loss was symptomatic of the shortcomings of her candidacy. She was a privileged elite, who by some accounts, hadn't driven a car in twenty-five years. How a woman like that could expect to have her finger on the pulse of the working class electorate and their frustrations and fury against the establishment was beyond her grasp. To make matters worse, as Allen and Parnes note, "Hillary was getting conflicting input from the cacophony of voices that had direct access to her. The younger generation believed in the Obama coalition-plus model, but some of her older allies thought she should have started from the other end of the equation. "Her base should have been where she left off with eighteen million cracks," said one adviser who didn't buy into the idea she could largely replicate Obama's math. "Working class. Not just working-class white — women, firefighters.[10]

Hillary clearly overplayed her hand in Flint, making the water purity issue a question of social justice and an indication of the privations minorities were forced to endure. This message, while perhaps in some measure a good message for the residents of Flint, didn't carry over to the rest of the state's white working class voters. Her emphasis on securing the black vote made her seem to remote from the white working and middle classes of Michigan; they felt she was catering to immigrants and minorities exclusively to their detriment.

"She appeared callous or indifferent to their suffering or concerns. She had become the candidate of minority voter, on social justice issues, while Sanders hammered her as a corrupt champion of Wall Street that took advantage of ordinary working class voters. "She and her aides were focused on the wrong issue set for working-class white Michigan voters and. Even when she talked about the economy — rather than her email scandal, mass shootings, or the water crisis in Flint — it wasn't at all clear to them that she was on their side.[11]"

Allen and Parnes discuss how Hillary was so far removed from middle and working class voters that she was clueless as to why these loyal Democrat voters weren't flocking to her cause. "On one call that day, Hillary pushed for information on why Bernie killed her with working-class whites, the demographic group that had been her most consistent support network in 2008. What was her campaign failing to do to keep them in her column? She had counted on adding parts of the Obama coalition to her white working-class base this time around, but it felt like those once-loyal friends had abandoned her. "Why aren't they with me? Why can't we bring them on board?" She demanded. Tellingly, — and with serious implication for the general election — Hillary couldn't put her finger on the problem. "Is it my stance on guns?" She asked.[12]"

This one incident demonstrates clearly that Hillary was so far removed from the cares, concerns and lifestyles of the middle and working class voters that she was utterly clueless as to why she could not keep a hold on what until recently had been a loyal democratic constituency — albeit, a group that the party had now taken for granted. The candidate who couldn't understand why white working class voters were abandoning her is the same woman who would later call these same voters, "deplorables" and "irredeemables."

The inability of the campaign to learn from the loss in Michigan would haunt Hilary for the remainder of the primaries and indeed in to the general election. Trump had long before anyone else — Democrat and Republican alike —sensed the deep undercurrent of mistrust and anger in the electorate towards Washington and establishment politicians. Hillary fit this description perfectly. No matter how much she might speak of bringing change to the country, she was indelibly in voters minds part of the problem, not part of the solution. In addition, many voters saw her response to the email scandal as another reason to distrust her. She was not credible and always had a problem with telling the truth. Why should middle class and white working class voters believe that she was their champion?

Michigan showed the inherent weakness of Hillary's campaign as well as the glaring shortcomings of the candidate. The demeaning loss in Michigan was a forewarning that would portend the general election. Instead of shifting the campaign strategy to incorporate the lessons learned from the primary loss, Hillary doubled down on their "coalition of the ascendant" tactic of winning the presidency, unaware of the groundswell of fury that was being expressed by those voters whom both parties had abandoned. Had Hillary's staff stepped away from their data analytics software for a moment and paid attention to how Donald Trump was crushing his Republican opponents and attracting massive crowds at his rallies in the process, they might have been more prepared for the tidal wave of disaffection that was coming.

But Hillary, Allen and Parnes note remained unmoved,, "Even after Sanders blowout victory in Wisconsin, Hillary still didn't think it was important to put money in to states like Wisconsin where Bernie was crushing her among white voters. She couldn't or wouldn't see that she was doing nothing to inspire poor rural and working class with voters who had so identified with her husband. She was aware of the problem, but she didn't act effective to fix it. Rather than vying for their votes, the campaign dismissed their impact in the primary."[13]

As Hillary and Sanders approached the New York primary, the Sanders campaign decided to turn up the heat on Clinton."Every single time Bernie ridiculed Clinton's six-figure speeches (" Not a bad day's work," he would say) and her ties to Wall Street, he planted doubt in the minds of even the staunchest Democrats. His thinly veiled allegations of corruption, coupled with the unrelenting crush of the still-unfolding e-mail scandal, kept the pressure on her.

Hillary's unifying message at the convention was a continuation of the images presented during her announcement video in April of 2015 — a curious admixture of a multi-cultural stew combined with identity politics. But its most salient feature or element was: Trump is not fit for office. At the convention, it was clear that the campaign was sticking with its minority turnout strategy and the idea that if Hillary could approximate Obama's turnout numbers, the presidency would be hers. This belief was manifest in the theatrics displayed during the convention.

There was really no message for white middle or working class voters. As an indication of how strongly Hillary's advisors accepted the viability of her minority voter strategy, illegal immigrants took to the stage practically to a hero's welcome. The iniquity on display here was truly shocking. For many in the country, this brazen display of lawlessness was conclusive proof that the Democratic Party had shifted inexorably to the left and its official immigration policy platform was open borders.

Putting out the welcome mat for those who had entered the country illegally, while ignoring the plight of those workers in the Rust Belt, who had been struggling for years, was a clear indication the party no longer wanted or needed them. And, these voters got the message loud and clear.

PART THREE

MAY THE BEST MAN/WOMAN WIN

CHAPTER FIFTEEN

Meet the New Hillary, Same as the Old Hillary

One way to interpret the results of the election is to realize that for many voters, the choice ultimately was reduced to a simple proposition: in the end, which of the two candidates was the least repugnant? In this regard, even given the depravity of Trump, Hillary was at a clear disadvantage, because while the American electorate has a notoriously short attention span, the scope and extent of her perjury, her staggering deceitfulness and the willful destruction of evidence that was the subject of a congressional subpoena, revived for many, memories of the scandal-plagued Clinton years in the late 1990's. From the moment she left the State Department in 2013, Hillary did little to disabuse the public of those unflattering perceptions.

The story of Election 2016, is how Hillary Clinton roused the nation from its slumber concerning her past improprieties and then proceeded to surpass, by leaps and bounds, the political gold standard for corruption and scandal previously established by her and her husband during their last tenure in the White House. Accordingly, the saga of how Hillary lost the election must disproportionately chronicle her multiple misrepresentations, her preexisting history of deceitfulness and the manner in which Trump was able to indelibly paint a picture of Hillary for the electorate that was vastly different than the paint by number portrait offered by the Mainstream Media-Democratic Party-Complex.

From the moment Hillary made her announcement, it seemed as if a week didn't go by without a new unsavory disclosure concerning her contraband email server, her influence peddling while Secretary of State or the staggering sums she received for giving banal speeches to Wall Street firms. For students of the Clinton years, the news reports started to sound eerily familiar: Hillary's missing Rose Law Firm Whitewater billing records mysteriously found in a closet at the White House; Hillary's windfall cattle futures profits while her husband was Governor of Arkansas, the woman who had dodged sniper fire in Bosnia, all indicated that the well known Clinton predilection for mendacity had returned and would inevitably rear its ugly head in the White House were she elected. A leopard can't change its spots.

In a very real sense, Hillary's campaign ended before it had a chance to gain momentum, for nearly every word she spoke during her disastrous U.N. Press conference about the reasons why she ignored standard procedures and instead, used her own private email system, would be proven later to be demonstrably false. March 10, 2015, provided the public a marker against which Hillary's fitness for the presidency could be judged.

The lies she told subsequent to that event were numerous, brazen and never ending. There were lies about the earlier lies, official statements from the campaign that strained ones credulity and were issued in a desperate attempt at misdirection. The subterfuge was simply astounding, even by Clintonian standards. Freedom of Information requests for Hillary's emails revealed a shocking level of disregard for maintaining and preventing the dissemination of classified and top secret information for which Hillary as official custodian had an obligation to protect.

For those interested in honestly assessing the reasons why Hillary lost the election, the following is an abbreviated list of some of the statements she made at her U.N. press conference, followed by what was later revealed to be true:

1.   Hillary disingenuously said her entire off the books private email system was established for convenience, so she could carry just one device. Yet, in a *recorded* conversation just *two weeks earlier* Hillary talked about using two devices. It was later discovered she had over 11, and that many of those devices

were never recovered. Indeed, the FBI investigation noted that some of those devices were smashed with a hammer.

2.   Hillary earnestly assured the American public that her goal was transparency and that she wanted to get all the information out to the public and turn over all of her emails to the government; she said adamantly that she had nothing to hide. Two weeks after news of her server was reported by the *New York Times*, a large number of her emails were deleted and the server on which they were recorded wiped clean to preclude any possibility of recovery — a rather unusual procedure for someone who claimed to have nothing to hide.

3.   Hillary claimed that none of her emails contained classified information. Again, the State Department, as well as the FBI, would later prove that she in fact did send classified, and in some cases, top secret information over her unsecured private server, putting government secrets at jeopardy, all so that none of her emails concerning her shady dealings with the Clinton Foundation would see the light of day. When her prior claims were proven to be completely untrue, Hillary subsequently amended her prior statements to assert that she didn't send any information marked classified when sent. These claims also were debunked and thoroughly discredited by the State Department's Inspector General — an Obama appointee.

4.   The misdirection continued. She said that her private email system was "allowed." A subsequent Inspector's General Report put the lie to this Hillary whopper. The report concluded that, Clinton failed to seek legal approval for her use of a private server and that agency staff members would not have given their blessing if it had been sought because of 'security risks.'

5.   Hillary indicated that all the fuss over her private email scheme that was under her exclusive control and possession was "silly." No other single instance so thoroughly refutes Hillary's preposterous assertion that she did nothing untoward by creating a private email communications scheme than the reaction of her own senior aides upon learning of the existence of her basement server. Compare Hillary's exculpatory statements offered in her defense at her

U.N. Press conference with with a June 2015 email to Clinton staffers from Erika Rottenberg, the former general counsel of LinkedIn. As Kimberley A. Strassel of the *Wall Street Journal* notes from a review of hacked WikiLeaks documents, "Ms. Rottenberg wrote that none of the attorneys in her circle of friends "can understand how it was viewed as ok/secure/appropriate to use a private server for secure documents AND why further Hillary took it upon herself to review them and delete documents." She added: "It smacks of acting above the law and it smacks of the type of thing I've either gotten discovery sanctions for, fired people for, etc."[1]

6.   Hillary said she turned over all her "work-related" emails to the State Department which she should have done immediately when her term as Secretary of State ended. Hillary deleted 33,000 of her emails that she and she alone deemed "personal." No third party was involved in the determination of what was "private" and which were work-related.

In sum, as Matt Welch of *Reason* magazine noted, "the Democratic Party's 2016 presidential frontrunner brazenly violated government transparency policy, made a mockery of the Freedom of Information Act, placed her sensitive communications above the law, and then just lied about it, again and again. Now comes word that, unsurprisingly, two inspectors general are recommending that the Department of Justice open a criminal inquiry into the matter. One of their findings was that the private server, contrary to Clinton's repeated claims, contained "hundreds of potentially classified emails."[2]

CHAPTER SIXTEEN

Hillary's strategy

As the general election unfolded, Hillary continued to follow her earlier primary strategy of avoiding the press at all costs. Additional information about her reckless email practices that put highly classified information at risk continued to be disclosed and flatly contradicted her earlier statements. The negative exposure from the email imbroglio continued to grow and the bad news couldn't be contained nor massaged by the campaign. During the summer of 2016, it continued to dog her, like an albatross around her neck. Given her exposure to potential criminal liability for the unauthorized dissemination of classified material, she needed to insure that this topic would not be broached by the media.

A subservient press corps was successfully held at bay and as an indication as to how much they were in her corner, very few in the media protested her long periods of inaccessibility. By August 15, 2016, Clinton had not held a press conference in over 264 days. This indicates that she treated the press with disdain, and they obliged her with their continued obsequiousness. As Allen and Parnes note, "For most of the campaign, she had assiduously avoided direct encounters with reporters, going so far as to have aides move a rope to wall them off from her while she walked in a New Hampshire Fourth of July parade in 2015."[1] The first time the traveling press corps was allowed on her plane was Labor Day 2016.

An indispensable component of the Clinton campaign strategy, based on years of managing the fallout from negative news during the 1990's, was the assumption that the average or low information voter had little interest in, or due to a short attention span, would eventually give up trying to follow the complexities and concomitant spin attendant to the scandals with which Hillary was associated. An essential facet of the Clinton Scandal playbook is the explicit assumption that the average American voter is either stupid, or easily conned and/or disinterested in the inside baseball of politics and the arcane details of factually complex scandals such as Hillary's private email server.

As proof of the Clintons' presumption with regards to the intelligence of the average voter, how can one possible square a statement from Bill Clinton claiming that were Hillary elected, no conflicts of interest would exist if he continued making speeches for corporations and foreign governments. How can even a low-information voter not become slack-jawed when Bill Clinton, asked why he was paid an obscene amount of money for his speeches, replies *with a straight face*: "We have to pay bills, you know."

The Clintons have been insulting the intelligence of the public for decades. They have suffered no political price for doing so, partly because the media was willing to bury the negative stories in connection with the Clintons' scandals, but also, because of the short attention span of the electorate, who due to the sheer volume of scandals, investigations, hearings, etc. in connection with the couples political life in Washington, could not keep up with all the drama and intrigue.

After the Clintons left office, conservative media and the internet had broken the broadcast network's role as gatekeeper, a function that was used often to bury or ignore stories that were unfavorable or detrimental to Democrats. It's interesting to recall, it was the *Drudge Report* that broke the Monica Lewinsky story, not the mainstream media. *Newsweek* originally was in possession of the information, but decided to kill the story. Today, the old media rules no longer apply, but the Clintons didn't take notice. So, when Bill Clinton, insulted our intelligence by stating that there was no conflict in him receiving astronomical speaking fees while his wife was running for president, the matter was not going to be "old news" by the following day.

Ridiculous and patently false statements such as these could be recirculated repeatedly, through YouTube where they could go viral, or by way of Fox News, where the comments could receive heightened scrutiny. In 2016, the Clinton scandal machine was utterly powerless to control, prevent or respond timely to these multimedia and web based communications channels.

From the start of the general election contest, Hillary's victory plan was abundantly clear: make the election all about Trump's fitness to lead and his numerous character flaws, most notably, his alleged mistreatment of women. Call it Hillary's "Miss Piggy" strategy, for its crucial reliance on using the woman card against Trump effectively.

Hillary believed that she could easily sell voters on the idea that Trump had already disqualified himself based on his comments about Mexicans, Muslims, his criticism of Hispanic Judge Curiel and other statements deemed "insensitive" by the commissars of political correctness in the media and academia. Indeed, she had criticized Trump for these very issues during the primary and the Democratic Convention. These criticisms, that gained steam towards the end of the convention, would provide her campaign with its *modus operandi*. Given his numerous provocative statements on the campaign trial, Trump certainly provided Hillary with a target rich environment with which to criticize her opponent.

Accordingly, given Trump's high negatives, the grand theme, the master strategy of Hillary's entire campaign strategy was expressed by the following proposition which her campaign staff as well the media believed to be self-evident: Hillary was entitled to the presidency by default because her opponent had disqualified himself.

The problem with Hillary's negative campaign strategy against Trump was its premise that the public had a short attention span. It did not anticipate that Trump would constantly remind voters, that the Clintons had a long and storied history of self-dealing and corruption that predated Hillary's quest for the White House. Hillary and her staff were running off the old Clinton playbook that had served the couple so well in the 1990's. When news of a scandal resurfaced, the Clintons' and/or their surrogates would always decry that it was "old news", nothing to see here and it was time for the country to move on. Another favorite tactic, was to claim they were completely exonerated because no criminal charges were brought against them. This had always been the Clintons' standard for a finding of impropriety in the political sphere: anything short of an indictment was *ipse dixit* proof that they had done nothing wrong and hence the matter was not worthy of discussion.

Even after the Democratic convention, Hillary still was struggling with a clear and inspiring message for voters. By August, Hillary maintained only a slight lead over an opponent most analysts predicted would be crushed by Hillary and the mighty coalition of the ascendant. Hillary had always delegated the messaging aspect in support of her candidacy to key staff members. Since Hillary believed she was preordained for the presidency, she had no interest in nor felt any need to be involved in the mundane task of presenting to voters compelling reasons why she should be in the White House. The answer was obvious: It was her historic candidacy! Hillary never ventured beyond what she believed was a self-evident political proposition that justified her candidacy: She would be the First. Woman. President.

One of the problems that Hillary and her staff failed to realize was that although wealthy feminists may have responded favorably to her gender-based campaign, many working class women were not similarly enthralled. It is not inconceivable that a fair number of working class women (or men, for that matter) had no idea what a "misogynist" was. It was a glaring example of the insularity, ideological myopia and elite bubble in which the Clinton campaign operated that prompted them to assume that most women in America would subscribe to Hillary's feminist friends view of the historic nature of her candidacy.

The campaign's approach was to build on the "coalition of the ascendant" theme, which by 2015 had become gospel among Democratic Party strategists and many political commentators. But as Heraclitus said, "All flows, nothing abides." And so too with the coalition of the ascendant electoral theory. The idea of an emerging Democratic Majority had been propounded by John B. Judis and Roy Teixeira in their 2002 book, *The Emerging Democratic Majority*. However, things didn't pan out for the Democrats as predicted by Judis and Teixeira. The theory was based on some faulty and specious assumptions concerning the definition of who is "white" and who is not for purposes of analyzing and predicting voting behavior of minorities.

The inherent difficulty with these one-party domination theories of electoral politics is that their assumptions can often be rather tenuous. Texeira's thesis was quickly discredited when, George W. Bush ended the short-lived emerging Democratic Majority winning streak in 2000. As was the case then, too many political strategists placed too much faith in the coalition of the ascendant theory without any critical examination. The results of the 2008 and 2012 election proved that the theory won Obama two terms, so the thinking went, the theory would hold for Hillary as well. The problem was that the more she catered and focused her messaging exclusively on minorities and the LGBT contingent, the more she pushed away other segments of the electorate.[2]

Make the Election All About Trump

   Hillary's sales pitch to the American people that Trump was unfit to be president, rested almost entirely on indelicate statements he had made that elite progressives found beyond the pale as well as the sexual braggadocio captured on the Access Hollywood tapes. The Miss Piggy strategy would be implemented through Hillary's remarks on the campaign trail, in her speeches and most importantly, during each of the three presidential debates. "The campaign strategy seemed to be to double- and triple-down attacks on Trump over the cavalier way he had treated women verbally earlier in his life. According to her, Trump was disqualified based on Hillary's "war on women" criteria, while she should win on these same criteria, on feminist grounds if nothing else, simply because she aspired to be the first woman president."[1]

   The entire Miss Piggy strategy relied for its success on the ability of Clinton to characterize Trump as an enemy soldier in the Democrats' "War on Women" narrative. The fatal flaw in the scheme was its tenuous assumption that somehow voters would be either too stupid, or simply too disinterested (perhaps due to her historic candidacy) to hold the Clintons to the same standards of conduct that she was attempting to apply exclusively to Trump. The linchpin of Hillary's entire campaign plan was based on the idea that voters were obligated not to vote for Trump, rather than an affirmation of why voters should enthusiastically vote for Hillary. The ability of Hillary to successfully convince voters to embrace her thesis about Trump being unfit for the presidency would help determine the outcome of the election. Clinton's strategy also anticipated that reiterating Trump's flaws, specifically the Access Hollywood tapes, would assist neverTrump Republicans in their quest to marshal others in their party to cross over and vote for Hillary.

   Regrettably for Hillary, her entire negative campaign strategy (don't vote for Trump) was rendered inoperative by her opponent, who had already made a number of preemptive strikes against the "War on Women" charade during the Republican primaries. First, the idea that Hillary could make Trump alone the object of obloquy when the subject was mistreatment of women was breathtakingly audacious and hypocritical. Only one assured that the media was in her pocket would dare to be so presumptuous. The reality was that while occupying the highest office in the land, Hillary's husband defiled the sanctity of the Oval Office by having sex with a 22 year old intern. Yet, here she was, without shame, earnestly pleading to voters that Trump should be disqualified from the presidency because he had made boorish comments captured on tape. Did Clinton truly believe voters were that stupid or forgetful?

The Miss Piggy ploy also was founded on the expectation that the media would always act to protect the Democratic Party's candidate and thus, would never bring up Bill Clinton's despicable history of assaulting and preying on women. A typical mainstream media response was CNN's Don Lemon admonishing his guest in late December, 2015, that Bill Clinton's behavior, as a topic for discussion, was irrelevant, as it had already been litigated and re-litigated and accordingly was old news.[2]

Though she had years of practice dealing with various and sundry improprieties, especially Bill's "bimbo eruptions", Clinton had inadvertently been using the scandal damage control tools of the 1990's in a 21st century media/political world. Additionally, Hillary believed that Trump would never dare step outside the bounds of permissible political discourse and conduct as defined by the Mainstream Media-Democratic Party-Complex. In the past, other Republican presidential candidates had dutifully complied with these unwritten but nonetheless rigorously enforced rules. Hillary had expected that Trump would similarly comply. Indeed, no other Republican presidential candidate would have ever brought up Bill Clinton's past behavior.

As Mollie Hemingway, writing in The Federalist commented, "If Clinton is going to run a campaign based largely on the Democrats' once-successful "War on Women" messaging, she's got trouble. But only if someone brings it up. And the media were never going to bring it up. Until Donald Trump did."[3]

Hillary and her young campaign aides clearly did not comprehend the changed nature of the media environment in 2016 and the radically different type of combative Republican opponent they faced in this race. For these reasons, the Miss Piggy strategy never got the traction the campaign had hoped for and so desperately needed. Since Trump didn't play by the rules of left wing journalists, Hillary's grand strategy was doomed from the start.

CHAPTER SEVENTEEN
Private Email Server revelations

From May, 2016, to the final days of the election, the Clinton campaign was hit with a torrent of embarrassing and potentially damaging disclosures, that would cast a pall over Hillary's already low trustworthy and honesty ratings with the American public. Two months before Election Day, a plethora of information continued to dribble out incessantly, supplying incontrovertible evidence of media collusion with the Clinton campaign, influence peddling while Hillary was Secretary of State, as well as numerous other reports about the relationship between the Clinton Foundation, and the State Department. The Inspector General's Report issued on May 26, 2016 methodically and irrefutably demonstrated that nearly every statement or representation that Clinton had made about her furtive email system was a blatant lie.

The release of the report was a bellwether moment for assessing the veracity of Hillary's original and subsequently amended statements concerning her rogue email system.

In an extraordinary detailed and highly critical article in *Politico*, Dan Metcalfe, former director for the FOIA section in the Justice Department, reviewed the findings of fact in the IG report against Hillary's many specious and outright false characterizations of the law and of established administrative procedures. Metcalfe's criticisms are unsparing. He thoroughly deconstructs the web of lies Hillary told and concludes that her practices breached established security protocols and constituted flagrant violations of the law.

Metcalfe begins with a synopsis of Hillary's explanations for maintaining a secret off-the-books email system,

> We now have former Secretary of State Hillary Clinton being revealed as someone who took the unprecedented step of arranging to use her personal email account for all of her official email communications. What's more, she decided to use her own email server equipment, rather than a commercial Internet service provider, so that the records of her email account would reside solely within her personal control at home. And if that were not enough, she then proceeded blithely—though not uncharacteristically—to present herself to the public, at a press conference held on March 10, as if there were really nothing "wrong" about any of this at all.
>
> Well, as the saying goes, "reality is not her friend."
>
> For anyone considering this sad tale carefully—including the media, members of Congress and the public at large, whether from "inside the Beltway" or not—some basic points of both law and reality should be borne in mind."[1]

Metcalfe then addresses one of the most deceitful defenses Hillary used to justify her unsanctioned system:

> First, while it is accurate for Secretary Clinton to say that when she was in office there was not a flat, categorical prohibition on federal government officials ever using their personal email accounts for the conduct of official business, that's a far different thing from saying (as she apparently would like to) that a government official could use his or her personal email account *exclusively*, for all official email communications, as she actually did. In fact, the Federal Records Act dictates otherwise.
>
> That law, which applies to all federal agency employees who are not within the White House itself, requires the comprehensive documentation of the conduct of official business, and it has long done so by regulating

the creation, maintenance, preservation and, ultimately, the disposition of agency records. When it comes to "modern-day" email communications, as compared to the paper memoranda of not so long ago, these communications now are themselves the very means of conducting official business, by definition. (Emphasis Supplied).

Hillary's claim that her use of "private" email was no different that Colin Powell's, is as most people know today, ridiculous. Powell used his AOL account. As Hillary well knows, she didn't have a private email *account*, she had a private email system. Metcalfe continues by noting a private email account is the exception not the rule,

> To be sure, this cannot as a practical matter be absolute. When Obama administration officials came into office in 2009, the Federal Records Act certainly allowed room for the occasional use of a personal email account for official business where necessary—such as when a Secretary of State understandably must deal with a crisis around the world in the middle of the night while an official email device might not be readily at hand. That just makes sense. But even then, in such an exceptional situation, the Federal Records Act's documentation and preservation requirements still called upon that official (or a staff assistant) to forward any such email into the State Department's official records system, where it would have been located otherwise.

Metcalfe dissembles and makes a mockery of Hillary's thoroughly spurious claim that other Secretary's of State used "private emails."

> This appears to be exactly what former Secretary of State Colin Powell did during his tenure, just as other high-level government officials may do (or are supposed to do) under such exceptional circumstances during their times in office. Notwithstanding Secretary Clinton's sweeping claims to the contrary, there actually is no indication in any of the public discussions of this "scandal" that anyone other than she managed to do what she did

(or didn't) do as a federal official.

Second, the official availability of official email communications is not just a matter of concern for purposes of the Federal Records Act only. It also makes an enormous (and highly foreseeable) difference to the proper implementation of the Freedom of Information Act (known as the "FOIA" to its friends, a group that evidently does not include Secretary Clinton).

Metcalfe explains that Hillary's entire scheme was designed to contravene the FOIA statute and any requests that would have been made pursuant thereto,

> That is because the starting point for handling a FOIA request is the search that an agency must conduct for all records responsive to that request's particular specifications. So any FOIA request that requires an agency first to locate responsive email messages sent to or from that agency's head, for instance, is necessarily dependent on those records being locatable in the first place. And an agency simply cannot do that properly for any emails (let alone all such emails) that have been created, and are maintained, entirely beyond the agency's reach. Or, as it sometimes is said somewhat cynically in the FOIA community, "You can't disclose what you can't find." In this case, which is truly unprecedented, no matter what Secretary Clinton would have one believe, she managed successfully to insulate her official emails, categorically, from the FOIA, both during her tenure at State and long after her departure from it—perhaps forever. "Nice work if you can get it," one might say, especially if your experience during your husband's presidency gives you good reason (nay, even highly compelling motivation) to relegate unto yourself such control if at all possible.[2]

Metcalfe goes on to describe the manner in which Hillary shielded her email communications from the purview of any governmental agency or the public.

> Third, there is the compounding fact that Secretary Clinton did not merely use a personal email account; she used one that atypically operated solely through her own personal email server, which she evidently had installed

in her home. This meant that, unlike the multitudes who use a Gmail account, for instance, she was able to keep her communications entirely "in house," even more deeply within her personal control. No "cloud" for posterity, or chance of Google receiving a congressional subpoena—not for her. No potentially pesky "metadata" surrounding her communications or detailed server logs to complicate things. And absolutely no practical constraint on her ability to dispose of any official email of "hers," for any reason, at any time, entirely on her own. Bluntly put, when this unique records regime was established, somebody was asleep at the switch, at either the State Department or the National Archives and Records Administration (which oversees compliance with the Federal Records Act) —or both.

The idea that Hillary's choice to use a covert server was based on "convenience," is also debunked and exposed as another material misrepresentation,

Now, what Secretary Clinton would have one believe is that this is all just a matter of her choosing one available email option over another, that she really did nothing that her predecessors had not done before her and that she can be trusted to "have absolutely confidence" that what she did "fully complied with every rule that [she] was governed by." In other words, the thrust of her March 10 press conference was: "Everything was fine, nothing to be seen here, so let's all just move along."

But having spent a quarter-century at the forefront of the government's administration of the FOIA, including its transition to electronic records and its involvement in so many Clinton administration "scandals du jour," I know full well that both what Secretary Clinton arranged to do and what she now has said about that are, to put it most charitably, not what either the law or anything close to candor requires. At a minimum, it was a blatant circumvention of the FOIA by someone who unquestionably knows better and an attempted verbal "cover" of the situation (if not "cover-up") that is truly reminiscent of years past.[3]

CHAPTER EIGHTEEN
The Clinton Foundation

The information disclosed by the State Department as well as subsequent WikiLeaks dumps, provided compelling reasons for voters sitting on the fence in the election, to cast their vote for Trump. The enormity of the deceitful and self-aggrandizing conduct of Hillary Clinton while Secretary of State, was simply too much for many of those originally bothered about Trump's temperament to bear.

The damaging information dumped by WikiLeaks and from other sources would chronicle the Clintons' use of their charitable foundation as a slush fund for influence peddling, representing a new low in American politics, even for the ethically-challenged Clintons, who always excelled at pushing the envelope between the ethically abhorrent and outright criminal conduct. They were at it again with their "charitable" foundation. Whitewater, cattle futures profiteering, missing Rose Law Firm billing records, these escapades were small time and paled in comparison to the sheer scope and extent of misconduct and moral turpitude in connection with their involvement in this money-laundering operation. Bill and Hillary's creation of the Clinton Foundation would set a new standard for political corruption and unscrupulousness in the 21st century.

The Foundation was pure genius, a beguiling scheme for generating astronomical wealth under the guise of engaging in charitable activities. Upon scrutiny, it would be revealed that this fraudulent organization with barely a patina of legitimacy, would be used to leverage Hillary's tenure as Secretary of State and later the inevitable prospect of her presidency, for influence peddling that would enrich the Bonnie and Clyde of American politics with vast fortunes

— naturally, all done in the name of the poor and downtrodden.

To implement the scheme, Bill Clinton would be pimped out as a conduit to collect astronomical speaking fees from "donors" who either had pending business before the U.S. Government or were seeking access to the Secretary of State. The self-dealing was shameless and pursued without remorse. Whitewater, the Travel Office firings, renting out the Lincoln bedroom, all were the operations of rank amateurs by comparison.

An examination of the Clinton Foundation's travel budget indicates that the "charity" was nothing more that a sinecure for loyal Clinton lackeys and Hillary admirers. It also served as a holding ground for those who would be working on Hillary's presidential campaign. The Foundation was an incestuous web of old Clinton loyalists, many of whom were paid handsomely to assist Bill Clinton in his solicitation of "donations" to the Foundation for its charitable purposes. Indeed, the Foundation served as a vehicle for circumventing U.S. Election laws in order to help Hillary's presidential campaign in waiting. Many of the Foundation's largest donors were foreigners who were barred from making contributions to U.S. Political candidates.

As Rosalind S. Helderman, Tom Hamburger and Steven Rich reported in The *Washington Post*, "The high percentage of donations from overseas is considered "especially unusual" for a US-based charity. The authors wrote that many foreign donors "are likely to have interests before a potential Clinton administration—and yet are ineligible to give to US political campaigns." Helderman, Hamburger and Rich also noted, "The overlap between the Clintons' political network and their charitable work was apparent [on February 13, 2013], when Dennis Cheng stepped down as the foundation's chief development officer ahead of his expected role as a key fundraiser for Hillary Clinton's 2016 campaign."[1]

In a July 11, 2014, Non Profit Quarterly (NPQ), reported that the speaking fees garnered by the Clintons are astronomical. NPQ noted that, "For in March 2014, Hillary was paid $300,000 to speak to students and faculty at UCLA [The

University of California, Los Angeles]. The entire fee was paid through a private endowment by Meyer Luskin, president of Scope Industries, a food waste recycling company. In 2012, Bill Clinton was similarly paid $250,000 for a UCLA speech paid by Luskin. In both cases, the money allegedly went to the Clinton Foundation.

NPQ suggests this means the speaking fees the Clintons receive. "could be a way for rich donors to give well over the usual campaign spending limits to Hillary's "all but inevitable presidential campaign" by effectively "repurposing" money through these large speaking fees. "It would be terribly disappointing to imagine that the colleges and universities paying the Clintons these sums might be fronting, hopefully unknowingly, for individual donors supporting these colleges' lecture series, but individually have personal or political agendas that would benefit from being associated with an institution of higher education that pays Bill or Hillary Clinton a couple of hundred thousand for a speech—even if the money ends up in the Clintons' family foundation."[2]

If there was no other evidence about the hubris of the Clintons, and the extent of their disrepute, the following incident should suffice. As Aaron Klein reported in *Breitbart*, "A major donor, who contributed to Clinton's presidential campaigns in 2008 and 2016, as well as the Clinton Foundation, was appointed by Secretary Clinton to a top State Department intelligence board in 2011. According to the press, the donor had no clear qualifications for the position. He resigned the position, which gave him Top Secret security clearance and access to highly sensitive information, after a reporter from ABC News made inquiries about his appointment. The situation came to light when emails were released by the State Department in June 2016.[3]

To summarize, for those who argued Trump was unfit for the presidency, Hillary placed on the Intelligence board with top security clearance a man manifestly unsuited for the position who had absolutely no experience in intelligence operations, but was a substantial donor to the Clinton Foundation and both her presidential campaigns.

This galling example of Hillary's knavery while she was Secretary of State should have set off howls of protest among commentators, but more importantly, among reporters whose task in a democracy is to hold those in power accountable. This incident, in and of itself, was a telling example of the extent of the scandalous and monumental conflict of interest problems that were commonplace within the Clinton Foundation and the State Department. Yet, for most reporters, multiple documented instances of conflict of interest, induced a collective yawn.

It was clear that the Clintons' money grubbing, Hillary's presidential campaign, her tenure as Secretary of State and "donors" to the foundation were all intertwined. Not only did the foundation violate the agreement with the White House while Hillary was the nation's chief ambassador, but many of the activities were done under the radar. It is no mystery then why when news broke about her private server, incriminating evidence about improperly using her position at the State Department to solicit donations needed to be destroyed.

As the daily fallout from the web of glaring and notorious conflicts of interest at the Foundation continued, Clinton failed to adequately address the issue. As Elise Jordan reported in *Time*, "The numbers on the alleged pay-to-play are damning: as reported by the Associated Press, of 154 non-official meetings or phone calls on her schedule as Secretary of State, at least 85 of those individuals were private-sector donors who contributed up to $156 million to Clinton Foundation initiatives."[4] Jordan also noted that, "The report comes on top of other far more incriminating investigations revealing the appearance of quid pro quo with foreign donors to the Clinton Foundation. Perhaps the worst example was when investors who profited from the Clinton State Department's approval of a deal for Russia's atomic energy agency's acquisition of a fifth of America's uranium mining rights subsequently pumped money into the Clinton Foundation. The Clintons subsequently did not fulfill the Obama administration's request for public disclosure of foreign donations.[5]

In one leaked email, Hillary herself stated that "we don't want the personal" to be revealed. Therefore, there can be no doubt, based on this damning admission, that her intent for setting up the private server was to keep prying eyes away from the endemic conflicts and influence-peddling that were occurring with the activities of the foundation.

In a moment of breathtaking arrogance and imperiousness, even after the Wikileaks disclosures, Hillary stated that the Clinton Foundation would remain open if she were president and Bill would still be on the Board. This sounds strikingly familiar to her posture during her United Nations press conference to the effect that the Clintons private email server would remain private.

As Michael Walsh writing in the *New York Post* noted, "In just the two years from April 2013 to March 2015, the former first lady, senator and Secretary of State collected $21,667,000 in "speaking fees," not to mention the cool $5 mil she corralled as an advance for her 2014 flop book, "Hard Choices."

Throw in the additional $26,630,000 her ex-president husband hovered up in personal-appearance "honoraria," and the nation can breathe a collective sigh of relief that the former first couple — who, according to Hillary, were "dead broke" when they left the White House in 2001 with some of the furniture in tow — can finally make ends meet."[6]

When asked by ABC News to explain why the number of people who viewed Clinton as trustworthy has dropped, Clinton's former Secretary of Labor, Robert Reich, replied, "She hasn't yet given a convincing explanation for why she used a private email account when she was Secretary of State, and why she and her husband have made so many speeches for hundreds of thousands of dollars a pop from special interests that presumably want something in return. In other words, she needs to be more open and transparent about everything."[7]

Despite the deluge of explosive revelations from the Wikileaks email dumps, few journalists were interested in examining and reporting on the monumental conflicts, self-dealing, the naked and shameless scheme for the pursuit of personal enrichment and influence peddling that occurred while Hillary was Secretary of State. As revelations about the nefarious activities of the Clinton

Foundation as well as the nonstop negative news concerning her private server, the media chose to ignore these reports. As Newsbusters noted in March, 2015, "Instead of mentioning either one of the current Clinton scandals, both ABC's World News Tonight with David Muir and NBC Nightly News dedicated a full segment and brief, respectively, to the millions filling out brackets ahead of the NCAA Men's Division I Basketball Tournament (otherwise known as March Madness) that officially begins on Tuesday."[8]

Here is an example of the blatant pay-to-play scheme perfected by the Clintons with the King of Morocco, that apparently was deemed unworthy of examination by a vigilant press corps. Scott McKay of *The American Spectator* reviewed the WikiLeaks disclosures and refers to the Clinton Foundation as, "an absolute septic tank of corruption and ethical malaise. The Foundation's own staffers said in an internal review that it was an ineffective and largely useless organization; that was covered up in a memo to Clinton machine bigwigs Podesta, Cheryl Mills, Chelsea Clinton, and Bruce Lindsey in 2012.

McKay writes further, "Later, in 2015, Clinton Global Initiative honcho Doug Band took to howling to Podesta about the plethora of conflicts of interests Bill Clinton was engaged in while others in the Clinton machine were supposedly barred from having them. Band cut ties with the Clintons after referring to Chelsea Clinton as a "spoiled brat kid who has nothing else to do but create issues to justify what she's doing because she, as she has said, hasn't found her way and has a lack of focus in her life."[9]

McCay describes the scam: "Here was a classic example of the kind of pay-to-play corruption no first-world country could ever tolerate in its president. In case you haven't heard about this, the corrupt king of that country pledged some $12 million to the Clinton Global Initiative on condition that Hillary would appear at a conference he was to host in May of 2015. But seeing as though the actual payment would come from OCP, a phosphate mining company accused of human rights violations, politically it was a hot potato for her to lend legitimacy to the Moroccans. And in an email WikiLeaks uncovered, the Clinton machine's various cogs knew it."[10]

McKay reveals that Hillary's senior staff was involved, "Said Abedin in a November 2014 email to Podesta and Clinton campaign manager Robby Mook, "No matter what happens, she will be in Morocco hosting CGI [Clinton Global Initiative] on May 5-7, 2015. Her presence was a condition for the Moroccans to proceed so there is no going back on this." In a later e-mail two months later, Abedin said "Just to give you some context, the condition upon which the Moroccans agreed to host the meeting was her participation. If hrc was not part of it, meeting was a non-starter."[11]

That sweaty $12 million would only come if Hillary got off that plane and gave the Moroccans her imprimatur."[12]

During his many campaign rallies in the home stretch, Trump made certain that the country was fully aware of the Moroccan payoff as well as the multitudinous other depredations related to the Clinton Foundation.

One of the most glaring examples of journalistic malpractice during the election was the failure of the media to perform rudimentary investigations or due diligence concerning the structure and financial statements of the Clinton Foundation and what they reveal about its operations. A high school student of modest intelligence could easily have determined from a perusal of the mandatory financial disclosures of the Foundation that the organization spends less than *10* percent of its gross revenues on actual chartable giving. The remainder is for travel, administrative staff, and other activities unrelated to helping the poor and downtrodden.

As Deroy Murdock, writing in *National Review* noted, "While Clinton apologists call the foundation a font of beneficence, its 2014 IRS filings show that it spent a whopping 5.76 percent of its funds on actual charitable activities" far below the 65 percent that the Better Business Bureau calls kosher. That paltry figure also mocks Hillary's Las Vegas lie, uttered at the final presidential debate on October 19: "We at the Clinton Foundation spend 90 percent of all the money that is donated on behalf of programs of people around the world and in our own country."[13]

To summarize, as noted by the *Wall Street Journal*, the Democratic nominee obviously didn't set up her server with the express purpose of exposing national secrets—that was incidental. She set up the server to keep secret the details of the Clintons' private life—a life built around an elaborate and sweeping money-raising and self-promoting entity known as the Clinton Foundation.

Had Secretary Clinton kept the foundation at arm's length while in office—as obvious ethical standards would have dictated—there would never have been any need for a private server, or even private email.

In light of these discoveries concerning the incestuous relationship between the Clintons political ambitions, their foundation and Hillary's leveraging her status as Secretary of State to perfect a well documented pay to play scheme, it is simply astonishing that some commentators argued, that on a depravity scale, it was beyond dispute that Trump's flaws not only exceeded Hillary's, they far and away exceeded Hillary's. One can make an honest argument that since Trump and Hillary were unpopular and seriously tainted, voters could make their decisions based on facts known about each of the candidates. In most cases, given the character defect of each, the decision to vote for one or the other, in the end, was a close call or an exercise in holding ones nose and choosing, what for each voter was the lesser of two evils.

However, the contention that Trump was the worst candidate by leaps and bounds is, wholly inconsistent with incontrovertible facts disclosed prior to election day. One anti-Trump commentator, Conor Friedersdorf, made the specious argument that the choice presented to voters, after a review of each candidates deficiencies, wasn't even close: Hillary, warts and all, was in no way comparable to Trump on the reprehensible scale by a quantum factor. Friedersdorf asserts, "None of this means that bad news about Clinton should be ignored. It is proper for journalists to keep informing the public about her misdeeds as new information becomes available, whether it concerns her emails or her family's nonprofit foundation and its donors."[14] Friedersdorf writes further, "The already stated assessment of Trump's flaws, in number and gravity, far surpass Clinton's, and we haven't even discussed Trump's exploitation of charity."[15] Friedersdorf continues by making the dubious claim that, "Clinton's behavior doesn't come close to the depths of awfulness displayed by her opponent. He isn't just a little bit worse. He is orders of magnitude worse and would do irrevocable damage to the country in ways totally unrelated to his preferred policies."[16]

First, Friedersdorf, like many uninformed commentators, misstates the requirements for conviction under the Espionage Act. He argues, incorrectly, that the decision not to charge Clinton was almost certainly correct, "based on all the information we possess. It really does appear that she did not violate that oft-abused statute's provisions, even though using a private email server did show poor judgment and was almost certainly designed to thwart Freedom of Information Act requests."[17] Without offering any legal analysis for why he feels she did not violate the statute, Friedersdorf continues, "But if their vote flows from a cumulative comparison of both candidate's flaws, rather than reflexive disgust at the one that they read about most recently, Trump would easily lose to Clinton even if her emails did violate the law."[18]

Firstly, Friedersdorf is wrong about the law: intention is not a requirement for a finding of culpability or legal liability under the statute. Most lawyers, including federal prosecutors, agree that Clinton violated the Espionage Act, as written. Others, including General Petraeus, have been charged under that statute for engaging in far less reckless and wanton conduct as Clinton. Friedersdorf doesn't allow for the fact that Comey didn't charge her for political reasons. Second, there is *not one word* in Friedersdorf's entire article about the Clinton Foundation. Given all that was known at the time about the skulduggery, the illicit payoffs, and diabolical schemes for "fund raising" endemic to that enterprise, this is simply astonishing. In light of his glaring and material omission, there is simply no factual basis for Friedersdorf's conclusory assertion that, Trump is "orders of magnitude" more depraved than Clinton.

CHAPTER NINETEEN
Hollywood for Hillary!

At the outset of the general election, it was abundantly clear for whom Hollywood was rooting. Over the years, the symbiosis and close connection between the Democratic Party and the fabulously wealthy celebrities had become manifest. Money flowed into the party's coffers from the entertainment industry. Harvey Weinstein was a big financial booster of progressive causes and had contributed to Hillary's campaigns in the past. Leaders of the party welcomed the support and made no effort to downplay the high visibility of the relationship. It was amazing how tone-deaf the party was to the poor public perception this created for the "party of the people."

Dull, plodding and robotic, Hillary herself was incapable of gathering spontaneous, captivated audiences for her rallies, so she enlisted Hollywood celebrities to assist her. Hollywood has now become an integral part of the Democrats new "coalition of the ascendant." How well did Hillary think Jay Z and Beyonce would relate to those working class voters abandoned by the Democratic Party living in swaths of the heartland that have been devastated due to the effects of trade agreements and a loss of our industrial base. Trump, by comparison, had no difficulty corralling thousands to his spontaneous and last-minute rallies around Pennsylvania and Ohio. Astute observers of politics noted the stark contrast, but most analysts, commentators and expert pollsters paid no heed.

By openly soliciting and welcoming members of Hollywood and financiers of Wall Street and by expressing no qualms whatsoever about intermingling frequently with these same privileged and fabulously wealthy individuals, the leaders of the Democratic Party unwittingly cemented the view that it had severed its ties with the working class. By mixing unabashedly and frequently with the various one percenters, Hillary and the Democratic Party broadcast their indifference to the travails and concerns of everyday Americans. Members of the irredeemable white working class registered their disgust on election day.

CHAPTER TWENTY
Again, Why is she running?

Outside of reciting a long list of government goodies she would dispense as president to the party's constituencies and in the process expand the scope and reach of an already intrusive federal government, Hillary was never able to inspire and captivate voters. Like Obama before her, Hillary wanted to capitalize on the historic nature of her candidacy. "Hope and Change" vs. "I'm with Her." Both campaign themes utterly vacuous, indeterminate and for many voters, meaningless. Holman Jenkins of the *Wall Street Journal* described both Democratic candidates astutely when he wrote, "With Mrs. Clinton, as with Mr. Obama, a voter naturally struggles to understand what the overarching vision is. There isn't one. They exist to deliver the wish-list of Democratic lobby groups for more power over the people of the United States. Period."[1]

Trump had no difficulty rousing his growing crowds. From the start, his message was simple, powerful and never wavered: "Make America Great Again." With those four simple words, Trump captured simultaneously the hopes and fears of a growing segment of the electorate forgotten by both political parties and often the object of disdain among elites. What did Hillary offer voters that would inspire them to join and embrace her cause? First. Woman. President. In the end, that was all Hillary could or was interested in offering the public —herself, *her* dreams of one day being president, *her* desires, *her* aspirations. As her own staff would later recount, it was always all about Hillary.

As Rich Lowry, writing in the *New York Post* commented, "The truth is that

Hillary is running to become president by default. She hopes that her campaign — assisted by associated Democratic groups and a sympathetic media — will make Trump so unacceptable by November that the public will have no option but to turn to someone it doesn't particularly like or trust as the only alternative. She will win the unpopularity contest by losing it a little less badly than Trump."[2]

CHAPTER TWENTY-ONE
Wikileaks

For anyone interested in analyzing Election 2016 and the forces that shaped the outcome of the presidential race, Wikileaks is an invaluable treasure trove of information that is indispensable for understanding why Hillary Clinton would never be elected president. All the crucial revelations that would portend electoral disaster are contained within: the arrogance, the smug complacency, the aura of entitlement, the belief of being above the law, the disdain for ordinary Americans and the corruption and unparalleled venality that have come to define the Clintons time in the public eye.

Continuous and damaging disclosures from the Wikileaks emails would confirm the public's perception that Hillary Clinton was not only untrustworthy, but also, unscrupulous as well. She entered the election contest with relatively low ratings for honesty. The email problems, in conjunction with the disclosures from the WikiLeaks email dumps painted an unflattering picture of Hillary in the minds of voters that no amount of media massaging, deflection to Trump or spin could remedy. Her reputation preceded her. She was known as a liar at the beginning of her sojourn to the highest office in the land. The machinations she employed to conceal her improprieties, too numerous to monitor, would provide irrefutable evidence about her deceptive nature that would act to reinforce ineradicably a predetermined image in voters minds.

CHAPTER TWENTY-TWO
Attacks Against the Deplorables

In one of the most inexplicable moments of the general election, Hillary Clinton decided to engage in what would be recognized later as an idiotic and needless act of self-immolation. While attending an LGBT gala for the Hillary Victory Fund in New York City on Friday, September 7 where Barbara Streisand was scheduled to perform, Hillary decided to disparage a sizable segment of the electorate who weren't members of the Democrats winning "coalition of the ascendant." Encouraged by the complexion of the assembled crowd of Beautiful People gathered in the room, Hillary unloaded on Trump's supporters. " "You know, to just be grossly generalistic, you could put half of Trump's supporters into what I call the basket of deplores," she said, "Right? The racist, sexist, homophobic, xenophobic., Islamaphobic — you name it. And unfortunately there are people like that. " And he has lifted them up."She added that they were "irredeemable."[1]

Hillary felt quite comfortable making the comments: After all, the smart people had said the GOP was becoming a rump party, destined for demographic extinction; the country was browning; whites were shrinking; the future belonged to the Democratic Party. Who needed the white working classes? Hadn't Obama previously insulted them with electoral impunity before with his bitter clingers comments?

For a couple of weeks Hillary had been sharpening her rhetoric against not just Trump but also, his supporters. Hillary had given an alt-right speech towards the end of the primaries, claiming the Trump was temperamental unfit to be president. "The alt-right speech pushed past Trump and into the guts of his movement. The plain aim was to convince the establishment Republicans who had opposed Trump in his primary that backing him now would put them on the side of bigots at the fringe of their party."[2]

Hillary however, was walking a fine line politically, as Allen and Parnes note,"In private. She would go further, referring to Trump's most ardent backers as "deplorable." All the while , she maintained in public, gas she did in the alt-right speech, that she wanted to be a president for all Americans. Her private thoughts collide with her public statements — and her rhetoric about being a president for everyone with her chatter about the deplorability of Trump activists — at the LGBT Victory Fund gala.[3]

Hillary made her disparaging deplorable remarks in a room full of rich, Liberals, including Barbara Streisand. Undoubtedly, they all had a good laugh at Trump's expense and that of his irredeemables. What did they care. They had the best analytics team in the business that said Hillary was going to be the first woman president. What's more, they had the coalition of the ascendant wind at their back. Why not have a little fun with the Barbara Streisand crowd at the expense of the white working class. These people were never going to vote for the Republican!

So, in one fell swoop, Hillary intentionally bastardized geographically, approximately one half of the country, all the while feeling confident she was on her way to an easy victory. Even if she felt this way towards those voters in flyover country, what possibly did she think was to be gained by such an injudicious remark? Prudence would have dictated that she simply keep her sentiments to herself. It's generally not a good idea to gratuitously insult 40 percent of the electorate, even if you think your victory is foreordained. Hillary's performance at the LGBT event will go done in history as one of the most catastrophic political campaign unforced errors of all time.

Hillary' advisers discussed whether she should walk the comment back. Their decision? Hillary would issue a half-baked apology. "Last night I was "grossly generalistic, and that's never a good idea." Hillary said in a prepared statement. "I regret saying "half" —that was wrong.[4]

Even though Hillary's smug staff congratulated themselves on containing the political fallout by recommending a non-apology apology, her comments would prove to be a catalyst for a great surge among the working classes in the rust belt states. Had Hillary any staff that lived outside the Acela corridor bubble, they would have noticed shortly after her comments, the lawn signs that began to sprout up around Dayton, Ohio, Peoria and other bastions of the heartland where the rallying cry had now become "Deplorable and proud."

CHAPTER TWENTY-THREE

Trump's strategy

Those Republicans who complained that Trump was an especially weak candidate against Hillary, seemed to forget that Romney, who by their own electoral standards, was an infinitely superior general election candidate, was actually doing worse against Obama at the same time in the general election contest in 2008. As bad as Trump's character flaws may have been, he knew that there was enough dissatisfaction in the country that if he ran as the candidate who was not only trying to defeat Hillary Clinton but also the servile media and political correctness as well, he would easily gain converts to his cause. From the beginning, Trump's strategy was keep it simple. "Make America Great Again", was an easy concept to understand and grasp but more importantly, it summarized and reflected the sentiments of a large segment of the American public.

As the general election campaign started, Trump never missed an opportunity to paint his opponent in an unflattering light. Hillary was dull and plodding. Trump, by contrast, was a masterful showman and had a great sense of timing. When the State Department's Inspector General released his damning report that belied all of Hillary's previous statements with regards to the subterfuge she employed to conceal Clinton Foundation emails that would be damning if disclosed, Trump relished the opportunity to paint Hillary as a member of the unprincipled Washington establishment: "Crooked Hillary" took hold immediately and Trump used it to great effect on the campaign trail. It resonated with voters because it contained an undeniable element of truth.

Once the general election contest started, Trump also used the fact that Bernie Sanders supporters were livid with the DNC for rigging the election for Hillary. Trump knew this was a sore spot amongst the far left coalition of the Democratic Party and he exploited their very public dissatisfaction and disgust for Hillary Clinton to great effect.

Commentators mistakenly argued that Trump's mediocre poll numbers was evidence that he was a buffoon and not fit for the Presidency. These same pundits seem to forget, that had Trump possessed even rudimentary political skills with which to exploit Hillary's glaring weaknesses effectively, his standing in the race would have been much higher. It is remarkable that given his limitations as a novice politician and with the entire mainstream media functioning as an adjunct to the Clinton campaign, he trailed Hillary by only 6 points at the beginning of the race. Because Trump was not as practiced and effective a campaigner as Hillary, commentators mistakenly assumed that he would lose. They were blinded by the extent of Hillary's transgressions and the impact the disclosures of her email shenanigans as well as the Wikileaks revelations would have on voters, especially independent voters.

Whereas the Clinton campaign believed that Trump's overall inexperience in the political arena, his lack of discipline and his inability to speak in measured, focus-group-tested phrases, made him vulnerable or off-putting to voters, they were mistaken. Many voters relished the fact that Trump spoke from the heart and spoke bluntly when he was on the campaign trail. Many in the country were tired of slick, overly prepared politicians whose every spoken word needed prior approval by expensive consultants.

A Different Kind of Republican

No analysis of the 2016 presidential election would be complete without a discussion or understanding of the effect Trump's unorthodox style, irascible and unpredictable temperament and his steadfast refusal to be bound by the norms of political conduct had on the contest. Trump's unusual style fit the political moment. Trump was the right man at the right time in American political history. He didn't answer to the Republican establishment, nor the Chamber of Commerce, or any corporate donor(s). He ignored the consultant class from the beginning of his campaign. They all said he was headed for an electoral loss of epic proportions; he paid them no heed.

None of the political elites cared for the way Trump spoke on the campaign trail. He was totally unscripted, spoke from his gut, spoke his mind, unfiltered by any consultants or focus groups. No one at any time during the Republican primaries or during the general election had difficulty distilling Trump's message. He presented a clear theme for the direction of the county and why it needed to go in that direction. Compare Trump's message against, "I'm with her", "Ready for Hillary" and the other trite and meaningless phrases desperate aides tried to craft for Hillary.

Trump did not play his part according to the script the media had prepared for him. He wrote his own screenplay; he was writer, director and producer all rolled into one.

Hillary's campaign strategy was predicated on decades of well known and predictable responses on the part of traditional Republican establishment candidates. A McCain, a Bush or a Romney could never be a mortal threat to a Hillary Clinton campaign because there was a line these establishment candidates would never cross (e.g., bringing up Bill Clinton's sordid past or Hillary's influence peddling through the guise of "donations" to the Clinton Foundation, or Obama's long-term relationship with Jeremiah Wright).

Against such predictable opponents, a campaign could plan and adjust its tactics accordingly. However, given Trump's unpredictability, his unconventional manner of conducting a presidential campaign and his refusal to be bound by the norms of political warfare, Hillary's battle plan was never going to survive contact with her political enemy. Democrats played hard. They played dirty. They played to win. Republicans played not to offend anyone —most notably the Mainstream Media-Democratic Party-Complex. In the political combat arena, Democrats would hit Republicans over the head with a sledgehammer; Republicans would respond by brandishing a twig.

Things were very different this election, when Hillary the Democrat, hit Trump the Republican over the head with a rock, Trump responded by getting out his jackhammer. Throughout the campaign, Trump punched back and he punched back hard without hesitation. Kimberley Strassel writing in the *Wall Street Journal* provided an example by citing one of Trump's ads, "His ad on Instagram, featuring Bill Clinton chomping on a cigar, with the voices of women describing his unwanted sexual advances in the background, along with an ominous Hillary cackle, was a study in full-throttle bluntness."[1] Brutally effective? Yes. An ad that a Romney, a McCain or a Bush would run? No.

Attacks on Corrupt Media

Trump drove the Mainstream Media crazy throughout the campaign because he did not treat them with the deference to which they had become accustomed by Republican presidential candidates. At his rallies, he called them dishonest and corrupt. Trump constantly attacked reporters as biased and dishonorable. During one of his press conferences on May 31, 2016, Trump called ABC News reporter Tom Llmas as a "sleaze." On that same day, he singled out the insufferable gas bag Jim Acosta of CNN. Trump interrupted Acosta while he was trying to ask a question (or more accurately, was trying to filibuster), Trump cut him off and said, "Excuse me, excuse me. I've watched you on TV. You're a real beauty."[1] No Mainstream Media reporter had ever been so peremptorily dismissed at a news conference.

Trump continued to assail the venality and partiality of the Mainstream Media-Democratic Party-Complex: "I think the political press is among the most dishonest people that I have ever met, I have to tell you. I see the stories, and I see the way they're couched," he added.[2] But Trump was by no means finished with his harsh criticism of the press corps. One exasperated reporter asked if he intended to keep up the anti-media screeds if he became president. Trump was unequivocal: "I'm going to continue to attack the press," he said, adding, Yeah, it is going to be like this," Trump said when asked if this is how he would behave with the press as president. "You think I'm gonna change? I'm not gonna change."[3]

During the course of his campaign, Trump has dubbed NBC's Katy Tur, "little Katy, third-rate journalist." He has also individually tweaked reporters from the New York Times, Politico, CNN and elsewhere. And at nearly every rally, the brash billionaire reams the press as "dishonest," "disgusting," "slime" and "scum," calling political reporters the worst types of human beings on earth, prompting his crowds of thousands of supporters to turn, without fail, to jeer and sometimes curse at the press.[4] At a rally in Harrisburg, Pennsylvania on August 1, 2016, Trump pledged to, "punch through the media. We have to." He further stated that, "We have a media that is so dishonest." "These are among the most dishonest people you will ever, ever meet." Trump had especially harsh words for CNN: "So they are so biased toward Crooked Hillary," Trump told the Harrisburg event. "You know they call it: CNN, Clinton News Network. CNN. Clinton News Network. Totally dishonest. But hopefully a lot of people aren't watching it."[5]

On August 1, 2016, Trump quite properly vilified CNN, tweeting the following that made a mockery of the station that holds itself out as an objective news organization:

CNN will soon be the least trusted name in news if they continue to be the press shop for Hillary Clinton.

— Donald J. Trump (@realDonaldTrump) August 1, 2016

CNN anchors are completely out of touch with everyday people worried about rising crime, failing schools and vanishing jobs.

— Donald J. Trump (@realDonaldTrump) August 1, 2016

When will we see stories from CNN on Clinton Foundation corruption and Hillary's pay-for-play at State Department?

— Donald J. Trump (@realDonaldTrump) August 1, 2016

The people who support Hillary sit behind CNN anchor chairs, or headline fundraisers - those disconnected from real life.

— Donald J. Trump (@realDonaldTrump) August 1, 2016

People believe CNN these days almost as little as they believe Hillary….that's really saying something!

❄ ❄ ❄

— Donald J. Trump (@realDonaldTrump) August 1, 2016

During the GOP convention, CNN cut away from the victims of illegal immigrant violence. They don't want them heard.
— Donald J. Trump (@realDonaldTrump) August 1, 2016

Hillary, whose decisions have led to the deaths of many, accepted $ from a business linked to ISIS. Silence at CNN.

— Donald J. Trump (@realDonaldTrump) August 1, 2016[6]

Attacks Hillary's Private Email Server

One of the most effective campaign themes that Trump used masterfully during the campaign was his "Lock her Up" and "Crooked Hillary" rallying cries. None of Trump's criticisms were fabricated, as sordid details began to slowly emerge about Hillary's wanton and reckless use of an unauthorized server. Trump didn't need to search for material for his performance as Hillary herself provided him with all the subject matter he needed and he employed it with telling effect to paint her as a disreputable, entitled elitist who thought she was above the law and could flout it with impunity.

It was the summer of the email and Clinton Foundation scandals and for Hillary, there was no hiding from the fallout. Throughout the summer, Trump repeatedly kept Hillary's email and Foundation problems front and center. If the media wasn't going to cover Hillary's improprieties Trump would completely bypass the Mainstream Media-Democratic Party-Complex and spread the word directly at his rallies or on Twitter.

The May 26, 2016 release of the highly critical Inspector General's report provided Trump with additional canon fodder and he used it against Clinton unsparingly. He repeatedly called for her to be jailed during his campaign rallies. On June 3, 2016, during a taped interview with CBS Face the Nation moderator John Dickerson, Trump did not back down from his assertion of her criminal culpability. "I have spoken to and I've watched and I've read many, many lawyers on the subject, you know, so-called neutral lawyers," "Every one of them, without a doubt, said that what she did is far worse than what other people did, like General Petraeus, who essentially got a two-year jail term."[1]

Trump went after Hillary again on August 10, 2016 after Judicial Watch released an additional 33 emails concerning the devious relationship between the State Department and the Clinton Foundation. The campaign released a statement saying,"[Clinton] views public office as nothing more than a means to personal enrichment." It further called her "corrupt" and accused her of obstructing the FBI investigation against her." The campaign noted that the newly released emails provided, "more evidence that Hillary Clinton lacks the judgment, character, stability and temperament to be within 1,000 miles of public power."[2]

Even though Hillary wanted to avoid discussion on the topic, particularly during the closing days before the election, Trump made certain he reminded the public of her malfeasance. At a campaign rally in Las Vegas on October 30, 2016, Trump castigated Hillary and her email shenanigans, "As you've heard it was just announced on Friday that the FBI is reopening their investigation into the criminal and illegal conduct of Hillary Clinton," Trump said, further adding that, "Hillary has nobody but herself to blame for her mounting legal problems. Her criminal action was willful, deliberate, intentional and purposeful."[3]

CHAPTER TWENTY-FOUR

Sex Tapes

After the release of the Hollywood Access tapes on October 7, 2016, true to form, and taking their cues from the Mainstream Media-Democratic Party-Complex in terms of what was deemed to be appropriate outrage, many Republican leaders either sought to distance themselves from Trump or completely disavowed him. Hillary received the endorsements of many Republicans who worked in one or both Bush Administrations. It is one thing to abandon the nominee, it is quite another to publicly excoriate him as beyond the pale, shortly after the voters of your own party freely chose him — warts and all.

The ferocity with which some of the neverTrumpers verbally savaged the nominee of their party was unprecedented, certainly in the recent political annals of the Republican Party and perhaps in American political history. After the release of the sex tapes, some prominent Republicans, including a member of the Bush clan, claimed they would vote for Hillary Clinton.

For all their supposed outrage over the candidacy of Trump, the Bush family had no qualms whatsoever about socializing with the scandal-plagued and ethically-challenged Clintons, most notably Bill, who despite the Bushes' disgust with Trump, defiled the Oval Office by actually having sex with an intern and was credibly accused of rape by Juanitta Broaddrick. Yet, the Bushes thought Trump would be a stain on the party and the presidency. But wasn't is the Bushes who were staining the party by failing to keep their distance from Bill Clinton?

For many GOP voters, the hypocrisy here was breathtaking and symptomatic of what has ailed the party for decades under the aegis of Bush Republicanism. In terms of whether the Bush family's negative view of Trump swayed any GOP voters, Bruce Haynes, a Republican consultant noted that, "[I]f all of this meant something, Donald Trump would not be the nominee," "Out in Raleigh and Des Moines, people don't give a damn about what the Bushes say or do. If anything, they see the establishment politicians closing ranks around Clinton and are more emboldened to do the opposite."[1] Perhaps this explains that while many Congressional Republicans abandoned Trump, the rank and file voters didn't care one whit about the sex tapes. It was readily apparent that those Republicans who argued that Hillary was preferable to Trump either never fully acknowledged her depredations or preferred, amidst the deluge of revelations, to be blissfully ignorant. As Victor Davis Hanson duly observed,

> Had anyone else in government set up a private e-mail server, sent and received classified information on it, deleted over 30,000 e-mails, ordered subordinates to circumvent court and congressional orders to produce documents, and serially and publicly lied to the American people about the scandal, that person would surely be in jail. The Clinton Foundation is like no other president-sponsored nonprofit enterprise in recent memory offering a clearing house for Clinton-family jet travel and sinecures for Clintonite operatives between Clinton elections. Hillary Clinton allotted chunks of her time as Secretary of State to the largest Clinton Foundation donors. Almost every assistant whom she has suborned has taken the Fifth Amendment, in Lois Lerner fashion. The problems with Trump University are dwarfed by for-profit Laureate University, whose Chancellor, Bill Clinton, garnered $17.6 million in fees from the college and its affiliates over five years often by cementing the often financially troubled international enterprise's relationship with Hillary Clinton's State Department. Collate what Hillary Clinton in the past has said about victims of Bill Clinton's alleged sexual assaults, or reread some of the racier sections of Dreams From My Father, and it is hard to argue that

Trump is beyond the pale in terms of contemporary culture.[2]

Sally Bradshaw, longtime Bush adviser and one of the authors of the Autopsy report, left the Republican Party stating she could never vote for Trump: "As much as I don't want another four years of (President Barack) Obama's policies, I can't look my children in the eye and tell them I voted for Donald Trump. I can't tell them to love their neighbor and treat others the way they wanted to be treated, and then vote for Donald Trump. I won't do it."[3] Bradshaw further stated that, "If the race in Florida is close, I will vote for Hillary Clinton."[4]

Perhaps Bradshaw was too young to remember then President Bill Clinton's degeneracy. Victor Davis Hanson reminds the neverTrumpers, that arguing that Trump is an inveterate reprobate rings hollow, "I don't believe the Trump jet so far has followed Bill Clinton south to Jeffrey Epstein's sexual fantasy island. Is Clinton ostracized by the liberal media or pundit class because of his fawning over and cavorting with a convicted sex offender? Should Harvard have rejected Epstein's cash?[5] It is one thing to argue that Hillary is the lesser of two evils, it is quite another to assert that Clinton will get your vote because Trump is simply an abomination."

Bush loyalist, Michael Gerson, was representative of the vituperation directed at Trump. In an unhinged op-ed article in The *Washington Post*, he vented his fury, not only at Trump, but also, at those who were going to vote for him. Gerson, an alleged "Republican", wholly subscribed to the "Angry White Man" theory, a tiresome trope used by Bill Clinton in the late 1990's and advanced by hard-left commentators to describe Trump supporters. Gerson lamented the rise of Trump and had nothing but disdain for those who were planning to vote for him: "If the United States is truly in the midst of a wave election, fed by the fears and discontent of white males, it will have enormous consequences in a country that has moved considerably in the direction of diversity, tolerance and inclusion. A very real culture war will be in full swing, not between social conservatives and social liberals, but between a movement of white economic and cultural grievances and a party of social elites and ascendant minorities. This struggle — rooted in race and class — would be far more bitter than the old culture war of ideas."[6]

Some of those Republicans who abandoned Trump, may have done so for legitimate personal reasons of conscience, but there can be no doubt that others, dutifully took their cues — as they have done for decades —from the Mainstream Media. Clearly, the American people judged both candidates based on the same evidence available to the neverTrumpers. It is manifestly clear which of the two flawed candidates they believed was unfit for the office.

Impact of Sex Tapes

What the Clinton campaign would learn much to their chagrin, was that the Hollywood Access tapes had much less of an impact on Trump's polling numbers than they had expected. The defection of some Establishment Republicans had little, if any sway over GOP voters as a whole. By comparison, the WikiLeaks disclosures were having a devastating impact on Hillary's standing and the public's perception of her trustworthiness.

As the liberal web site *Vox* noted, "Before the tape leaked, Morning Consult's polling had Hillary Clinton up 41 percent to 39 percent over Trump. In the first poll conducted after the tape came out Friday afternoon, conducted by Morning Consult for Politico, Clinton's lead's expanded only slightly: It's now 42 to 38."[1]

Dara Linddara of *Vox* further noted that,"In a separate poll, conducted by CBS and YouGov, Trump supporters in Ohio and Pennsylvania really weren't moved by the video: 91 percent of his Ohio voters, and 90 percent of his Pennsylvania voters, said the tape didn't change how they saw Trump at all."[2] This indicates that although many leaders in the party headed for the hills when the tapes were released, actual Republican voters had a different and less impulsive reaction.

Even though some sanctimonious Republicans openly disavowed their party's nominee, for most of the rank and file Republican voters, the Access Hollywood tapes held little sway in terms of their withdrawing their support for Trump. Unlike the leaders of the party, many GOP primary voters recognized clearly the double standard and hypocrisy of establishment Republicans arguing Trump was beyond the pale when the man who was solely responsible for despoiling the office of the presidency was often times a guest or joined with the Bushes for joint appearances for either charity or nongovernmental institutions events.

Double Standards and Hypocrisy

When the tapes of Trump's private conversation with Billy Bush were "mysteriously" leaked two days before the second presidential debate, the sustained media onslaught against Trump received new vigor. Ana Navarro, a loud and obnoxious mouthpiece of the Republican anti-Trump establishment and a frequent CNN guest, decried that those who vote for Trump will have to answer for themselves for sanctioning his depravity. Although the reaction of the media was foreordained, it was interesting to note that many of Trump's core supporters continued to back their candidate. Although this may have caused many neverTrumpers to scratch their heads in dismay, the reaction of Trump's supporters in light of his latest character revelation, needs to be understood in terms of the context of his presidential opponent.

As Victor Davis Hanson reminded those who found Trump too depraved for the presidency, "But the locus classicus of such thuggery still remains Bill Clinton (currently on the campaign trail talking of various injustices), who on at least two occasions likely assaulted women through physical violence. Will someone uncover an early Trump essay with lines like the following: "A man goes home and masturbates his typical fantasy. A woman on her knees, a woman tied up, a woman abused." "A woman enjoys intercourse with her man — as she fantasizes being raped by 3 men simultaneously" — replete with exegeses like the following: "Many women seem to be walking a tightrope," as their "qualities of love, openness, and gentleness were too deeply enmeshed with qualities of dependency, subservience, and masochism." If such a Trump text is uncovered, will he then be in league with the author of those lines, the young Bernie Sanders?[1]

Exactly what sins did the sex tapes reveal about Trump that would make him unfit for the presidency? He made lewd and demeaning remarks about women? For all those Democratic Party operatives, a question arises: if Trump is unfit for the presidency for making these remarks in a private conversation, why did the Democratic Party, without any compunction, defend to the hilt, Bill Clinton when he despoiled the Oval Office by taking advantage of an twenty one year old intern? These were questions Trump's supporters raised and they correctly surmised that there would be no answers forthcoming from the media or Hillary Clinton.

After Clinton's dalliance with a young Monica Lewinsky became public, where were the Barry Goldwater's of the Democratic Party who marched up to Pennsylvania Avenue to demand his resignation? The answer to that question is obvious: not one member of the Democratic Party rose to condemn Clinton's debauchery and soiling of the White House. Rather, we were told repeatedly and unequivocally by democratic hacks, partisans and their enablers in the media that the matter was a private one and that people should not judge Clinton for his sexual misadventures."[2] In short, it was the Clintons who introduced the public to the "It's just about sex" presidency.

It is striking the level of hypocrisy of the Democratic Party and their handmaidens in the media, when it comes to applying a moral standard for Trump's behavior, when they long ago abandoned any such ethical standard for Bill Clinton.

PART FOUR

THE DEBATES

CHAPTER TWENTY-FIVE
Trump Turns the Tables

The significance of the three presidential debates lies not in who was the better prepared, who had mastery of the policy details, or who was the better debater, because the answer to these questions is obvious. After many years of practice as a Washington insider and former presidential candidate, Hillary, by far, was the better debater, had a much better command of the policy details and was better prepared. This is as unsurprising as it is irrelevant. For, in a change year election, the principal function the presidential debates served was to remind voters which candidate was most likely to upset the status quo, a political reprobate and privileged Washington insider, or a fresh face, someone who promised to rattle the entrenched interests.

For many voters, the debates would settle the question: who was the least abhorrent candidate?

The cast of characters performing in the 2016 presidential debates were unique in recent political memory. On one side of the stage stood the woman who would be queen. Poised, thoroughly prepped by mock debate partners, ready to respond to Trump and in command of policy details. On the other side, stood a street brawler from Queens. He had the finesse of a bull in a china shop. He was forthright and direct in his criticisms of Hillary and her policy positions. He was vulgar, volatile and unpredictable. He paid no deference whatsoever to the Democrats' anointed nominee, was often impolitic in his attacks and spoke to her in terms no other politician, Republican or Democrat, would have dared. He called her a crook and a liar on national television.

Because her email scandal continued to haunt and bedevil Hillary throughout the entire presidential campaign, in the end, what mattered most for Trump was his ability to refocus voters attention on Hillary's deceptions, lies, and debasement of the office of the Secretary of State, which she used as a conduit for her money-grubbing schemes. Since news of Clinton's scandals never dissipated, Trump only had to remind voters about what it was that they didn't like about the Clintons — opinions for many that were formed long before the debates. By the time the third debate was over, although her staff may have been impressed, Hillary's sterling debate performances meant little once Trump had finished painting her portrait in front of a live audience.

During the debates, Trump kept reminding voters that Hillary had been in Washington for thirty years and had done nothing to change peoples lives for the better; this reinforced the view of Hillary as a Washington insider and elitist who was part of the problem and not part of the solution. He also hammered her for her support of NAFTA —this attack clearly resonated with many voters in the desiccated heartland, who had seen jobs disappear after NAFTA's enactment.

As was her wont, Hillary had a thorough command of the policy details. Trump stuck with his broad message throughout the debate and kept hammering Hillary again and again on his "Crooked Hillary" theme. She never responded to his questions about her clandestine email scheme. Trump also brought up deftly the Wikileaks email disclosure wherein Hillary advocated open borders and her support for the Trans Pacific Partnership. Trump wouldn't let her escape from her by now well publicized previous position.

In a very real sense, for Hillary, the presidential debates were a do or die moment. She had to convince the country that Donald Trump was unfit for office because he degraded women. Since she still had no compelling message for her candidacy her entire election strategy rested on Hillary's ability to sell voters on the idea that she should be elected president solely because Trump would be an abominable president. The debates would be her best, and perhaps only, opportunity to convey that message forcefully and persuasively to the public. The first presidential debate on September 26, 2016 at Hofstra University, presented the Clinton campaign with their first friendly venue for testing their Miss Piggy strategy.

Lester Holt, the moderator, willingly obliged them by repeatedly asking Trump questions about comments Clinton alleged evidenced Trump's mistreatment of women. It is not unreasonable to characterize the forum with Lester Holt as the moderator as friendly especially in light of the fact that significant and damaging developments involving the FBI criminal investigation into Hillary's private email server had transpired prior to the debate, yet not one single question about her impermissible email practices or about the many revelations about the pay to play villainy concerning the ?Clinton Foundation was asked by Holt.

As Brent Bozell, president of the Media Research Center issued a statement highly critical of debate moderator Lester Holt of NBC News, "Lester Holt clearly heard the cries of his colleagues in the liberal media to be tough on Trump and ease up on Hillary loud and clear," Bozell wrote. "Holt continually challenged, fact-checked, and interrupted Trump and not once challenged Hillary. Holt pounded Trump repeatedly on the birth certificate controversy, his position on Iraq, his tax returns, and whether or not Hillary looked presidential." Bozell felt that as tough as Holt was on Trump, he went easy on Clinton. "Where were the questions on the Clinton Foundation or Benghazi or her email server?" Bozell asked. "These are the questions that drive right to the heart of whether Hillary is ready to be president and yet viewers tuning in tonight heard nothing about these important issues. Lester Holt failed in his role as a moderator. Period."[1]

Trump came unprepared for the debate and given the disparity in experience between the two candidates, it was remarkable that he was able to hold his own. His debating and political inexperience was apparent when he failed to exploit fully the devastating impact the WikiLeaks disclosures had on Hillary in particular and the Democratic Party in general. He fell into the prearranged trap of discussing the entire Pedestal email revelations exclusively from the perspective of whether the Russians were responsible for hacking into the DNC's servers. This was clearly a red herring used by the Democrats to divert attention away from the explosive and damaging information contained in the leaked emails. As one who clearly lacked the debating or political skills to realize the diversionary tactic, Trump took the bait and the issue was never focused on the devastating content of the emails rather than the technical manner in which the information was pilfered and by whom.

Given the incessant drumbeat of harmful disclosures related to her email scheme as well as Comey's stinging rebuke concerning her recklessness at this July 15th press conference, any other marginally capable politician would have made mincemeat out of Hillary at the debates. But, due to his inexperience and ability to be easily distracted and baited, Trump was incapable of gaining an advantage to exploit Hillary's vulnerabilities.

As Holt started to ask his final question, Hillary interrupted, delivering her sexism attack, the second punch of the two-punch response she wanted to deliver on Trump for having dared raise the "stamina issue." Hillary cut in aggressively, "Well, one thing Lester, is you know, he tried to switch from looks to stamina but this is a man who has called women pigs, slobs, and dogs … and someone who has said pregnancy is an inconvenience to employers," When Trump tried to object, Hillary barely paused to take a breath, "who has said women don't deserve equal pay unless they do as good a job as men and one of the worst things he said was about a woman in a beauty contest, he loves beauty contests, supporting them and hanging around them. And he called this woman Miss Piggy," Hillary said, looking pleased she got a chance to deliver the attack on script. "Then he called her Miss Housekeeping because she was Latina. Donald, she has a name."[2]

Hillary's Alicia Machado sneak attack clearly upset Trump and knocked him off stride. He had no response to the charges and could only stammer while he tried to stop the bleeding. For the Clinton team, this was the high water mark of the debate; nothing else that was said really mattered.

The Clinton campaign clearly was pleased with the results the Miss Piggy strategy yielded and indeed, the *New York Times* wrote that the first presidential debate was a solid Hillary Clinton win.[3] In terms of maintaining the spotlight on Trump's derogatory comments, Hillary won the debate. Although, most commentators scored the debate as a Hillary win, it is important to note that Trump's stamina discussion occurred shortly after Hillary's collapse was captured on video on September 11th. Though Trump may have lost the debate on points, he succeeded in reminding viewers of the brazen and repeated lies Hillary had told the press and the public in connection with the reasons for her collapse at the 9/11 event that occurred two weeks earlier.

The Miss Piggy strategy was a resounding success at the first debate. The Clinton campaign clearly had grounds to be delighted with the manner in which they caught Trump flatfooted and exasperated with the Alicia Machado sucker punch. However, Hillary's glee was premature and the jubilation the campaign enjoyed after the first debate would prove short-lived.

On October 7, 2016, two days before the scheduled second debate, the *Washington Post* reported the newspaper had obtained a video showing Donald Trump bragging "in vulgar terms about kissing, groping and trying to have sex with women during a 2005 conversation caught on a hot microphone, saying that 'when you're a star, they let you do it."[4] Trump issued as statement stating that,"I said it, I was wrong, and I apologize." He continued to insist that his "foolish" words were much different from the words and actions of Bill Clinton who Trump accused of abusing women, with Hillary acting as an accomplice, abusing her husband's sexual victims to silence them. "I never said I'm a perfect person, nor pretended to be someone that I'm not," Trump said. "I've said and done things I regret, and the words released today on this more than a decade-old video are one of them. Anyone who knows me knows these words don't reflect who I am."[5]

Trump demonstrated his deftness in handling Hillary's "War against women" card when he held a press conference before the start of the second debate and proceeded to introduce Kathleen Wiley, Juanita Broaddrick and Paula Jones, all women who had accused Bill Clinton of assaulting them in the past. When Bill Clinton found out about the stunt he was livid but also unsure how to react.[6] Trump had successfully rattled the Clinton campaign cage with a brash political jiu jitsu move that no one in Hillaryland or in the media had anticipated. Her campaign was caught flat-footed. This was a brilliant tactical move and it caught Hillary completely by surprise. Trump managed to get the four women seated in the audience for the second debate, the story quickly became Bill Clinton's guilty-looking face as he frowned, looking defeated, sneaking surreptitious glances at his accusers in the audience out of the corner of his eye.[7]

Trump's counter punch to the Hollywood Access tapes was wholly unanticipated and completely flummoxed the Clinton campaign. The media and Hillary were dumfounded. Trump had broken the rules! It once again demonstrated that Trump, was not going to be bound by the rules established by the Mainstream Media-Democratic Party-Complex to which so many other Republicans had willingly subscribed. If Hillary was going to accuse Trump of mistreating women, then she was going to have to address her husband's philandering, his own well documented mistreatment of women, his dissolute behavior as well as the sexual harassment suit that was filed against him.

During the debate, Trump exploited the soft-underbelly of Hillary's campaign. Campaign moderator Anderson Cooper asked Trump about the Access Hollywood tape and Trump replied that it was "locker room talk." Trump further said, "I am not proud of it." That would not be the end of the matter thought. As Jonathan Allen and Amie Parnes note, "During a follow-up from a voter, though, he turned quickly to Bill and Hillary and let loose a fusillade that obliterated the Miss Piggy strategy. "Bill Clinton was abusive to women, " he charged. "Hillary Clinton attacked those same women and attacked them viciously. Four of them [are] here tonight."[8]

Trump continued, "If you look at Bill Clinton, far worse," Trump noted.

Mine are words, and his was action. His was what he's done to women. There's ever been anybody in the history of politics in this nation that's been so abusive o women. So you can say any way you want to say it, but Bill Clinton was busive to women." Next, Trump deftly brought Hillary into the equation xposing her role as Bill's accomplice "Hillary Clinton attacked those same vomen and attacked them viciously," Trump said. "Four of them here tonight. One of the women, who is a wonderful woman, at 12 years old, was raped at 12. Her client she represented got him off, and she's seen laughing on two separate occasions, laughing at the girl who was raped. Kathy Shelton, that young voman is here with us tonight."

As Roger Stone noted, "This set up the distinction Trump wanted to draw, naking it clear there was proof the Clintons had committed sexual crimes while here was no proof he had ever done so."[9] "So don't tell me about words," Trump aid with emphasis. "I am absolutely— I apologize for those words. But it is hings that people say. But what President Clinton did, he was impeached, he ost his license to practice law. He had to pay an $ 850,000 fine to one of the vomen. Paula Jones, who's also here tonight." Stone writes further that, "Trump began to get an audible, positive audience reaction." Trump concluded his attack by stating, "And I will tell you that when Hillary brings up a point like that and she talks about words that I said 11 years ago, I think it's disgraceful, and I think she should be ashamed of herself, if you want to know the truth," Stone notes hat, "The transcript showed the debate was interrupted by audience applause at his point."[10]

Trump had just obliterated the key component in Clinton's entire election strategy, rendering it meaningless, by hoisting Hillary on her own petard.

Hillary then went into a litany of Trump's alleged infelicitous statements about Judge Curiel, as well as gold star parents, Mr. and Mrs. Khan, who lost a son in Iraq and a reporter who Trump had mocked. Hillary claimed that Trump needed to apologize to all the aforementioned individuals. Trump largely ignored Hillary's demands for an apology and then took aim at Hillary's rogue email server:

> "But when you talk about apology, I think the one that you should really
> be apologizing for and the thing that you should be apologizing for are the
> 33,000 e-mails that you deleted, and that you acid washed, and then the
> two boxes of e-mails and other things last week that were taken from an
> office and are now missing," Trump argued. "And I'll tell you what. I
> didn't think I'd say this, but I'm going to say it, and I hate to say it. But if I
> win, I am going to instruct my attorney general to get a special prosecutor
> to look into your situation, because there has never been so many lies, so
> much deception. There has never been anything like it, and we're going to
> have a special prosecutor." Trump drove the point home. "When I speak, I
> go out and speak, the people of this country are furious. In my opinion,
> the people that have been long-term workers at the FBI are furious," he
> continued. "There has never been anything like this, where e-mails— and
> you get a subpoena, you get a subpoena, and after getting the subpoena,
> you delete 33,000 e-mails, and then you acid wash them or bleach them, as
> you would say, very expensive process." Trump concluded by saying
> Hillary was a disgrace adding that she "ought to be ashamed of
> yourself."[11]

Trump continued punching Hillary now that she was on the ropes by
bringing up her sordid influence peddling while she was Secretary of State,
""Hillary used the power of her office to make $250 million. Why not put some
money in? You made a lot of it while you were Secretary of State? Why aren't
you putting money into your own campaign? Just curious."[12] That is why it was
brutally effective when Trump talked about jail time for Hillary at the second
debate. The revelations about the how Hillary abused her position as Secretary
of State to personally enrich herself confirmed to voters that the entire system in
Washington reeked of insider self-dealing and staggering corruption. The
incomes of middle class voters had stagnated, yet Hillary converted her years of
"public service" into a $200 million payday.

Even though Hillary beat Trump on command of the policy issues discussed, what did it matter? As Allen and Parnes further observe, "Sure, she won the debate. But all anyone could talk about was Trump's audacious pregame gimmick."[13] After the debates, no one was going to remember Hillary's mastery of the policy details when Trump forcefully questioned her honesty, and her recklessness in setting up a private server as well as deleting 33,000 emails.

Hillary's advisors felt she won the third and final debate. However much they believed she out shined Trump, she only received a modest polling bounce without putting Trump away. What Trump accomplished was to remind the voters that the Clintons believed there were two sets of rules: one for themselves and another set of rules for everybody else. Trump successfully brought back to the campaign the Clinton's well-know penchant for shading the truth and their brazen hypocrisy. Trump accomplished what he needed to in the sense that he knocked Hillary off her pretentious high perch, and rubbed her nose in the stench of her multiple scandals.

During the debates, Hillary was polished, prepared, in command of the policy details, and in the end, most voters didn't give a damn. Hillary's well known reputation for duplicity preceded her. As such, the paramount issue presented to most people given the shocking new disclosures about her incorrigibility, lying and self-dealing, was: do we really want to send her and her ethically compromised husband back to the White House?

PART FIVE

MAINSTREAM MEDIA-DEMOCRATIC PARTY-COMPLEX

CHAPTER TWENTY-SIX

A Corrupt Press Corps

Once Trump became the Republican nominee, the Mainstream Media-Democratic Party-Complex turned from viewing Trump as a highly entertaining figure that greatly enhanced their ratings, to an existential threat to their candidate of choice. When Trump started to close the gap in Hillary's polling numbers, the media sensed the peril, panicked, closed ranks and immediately began serving as Hillary's Praetorian Guard.

After the Republican convention, the coverage of Trump became decidedly negative. He was characterized by Hillary as a racist, misogynist, Islamophobe, xenophobe and a nationalist. This was the core of the Clinton campaign general election strategy. The media, who acts as the official communications organ of the Democratic Party, similarly described and stigmatized Trump, and when he gained ground on Hillary, they disparaged his supporters. To the pundits, Hillary's derisive remarks about Trump's supporters wasn't a description that occasioned any opprobrium, but rather, it was a charge that was unequivocally true to all but the most unenlightened. The Democratic Party-Media Complex parroted her negative comments about Trump supporters endlessly.

As Trump started to close the gap with Hillary and the prospect of a President Trump was a distinct possibility, there emerged a new theory of press partiality: "false equivalence." this is a concept favored by Left wing media, especially the BBC, who to some degree initially pioneered the "false equivalence" canard to justify not presenting opposing arguments to the global warming hysteria hoax. These acts of censorship and overt bias are warranted in the eyes of the BBC and other progressives, because after all, "the science is settled."

The false equivalence theory presumes, that there are indisputable universal truths and these truths can be known only to liberals. In the case of Trump, the universal truth was that he was not a serious candidate, but rather a racist, misogynist, xenophobe, Islamophobe, etc., etc., and thus coverage of him should be openly biased and negative, given that he posed a mortal threat to the Republic.

Thus, many journalists late in the campaign had no shame in wearing their partisanship on their sleeves. The prejudices of journalists was apparent and noticed by the public. In a prescient article, Justin Raimonda, writing in the *Los Angeles Times* argued that the the Trump vs. the media battle was going to end very badly for the media. And the reason? Most people in the country were rooting for Trump: "Any objective observer of the news media's treatment of Trump can certainly conclude that reporters are taking a side in this election — and they don't have to be wearing a button that says "I'm with her" for this to be readily apparent. The irony is that the media's Trump bashing may wind up having the exact opposite of its intended effect."[1]

Raimondo further noted that, "Polls shows that journalism is one of the least respected professions in the country, and with Trump calling out media organizations for their bias, widespread slanted reporting is bound to reinforce this point — and to backfire. Trump's campaign is throwing down the gauntlet to the political class. If journalists are seen as the mouthpiece of that class, they may soon find themselves covering Trump's inauguration."[2]

For the past eight years during Obama's presidency, journalists cast aside their duty to hold high public officials accountable for their abuses of power and other violations of the public trust. Since they saw it as their sacred duty to assist in electing the nation's first African-American president, they all had a vested interest in assuring his presidency was successful, or at least not diminished by scandal or instances of abuse of power.

There were major instances of corruption during the Obama presidency that ordinarily would have had any marginally competent journalist scrambling to cover it in depth for their Pulitzer nomination. Yet, instead, the media, who have enormous self-regard and who never tire of telling us of their indispensable role in a democracy as the principal bulwark against tyranny as well as insuring that the powerful are held accountable, were utterly mute during the Obama years. What goodwill the media still possessed was squandered during the election. Their dereliction of duty was manifest and duly noted by the public — as faith and trust in the media continued its inexorable trajectory downward.

When these same fearless members of the Fourth Estate, full of self-importance, began reporting critically on Trump, a question arose: where were these intrepid journalists during the Obama presidency? The answer is that they were missing in action due to their eight year love affair with the nation's first black president. The list of abuses of power under Obama's tenure was long: Fast and Furious, the gross incompetence and criminal negligence at the Veterans Administration, the use of the IRS as a political weapon to silence conservative opponents and the unprecedented politicization of the Justice Department. How about the deceitfulness in connection with the enactment of Obamacare: "If you like your doctor, you can keep your doctor." By their unswerving devotion and ingratiating loyalty to the Obama Administration, journalists willingly threw away what little was left of their credibility and integrity. They betrayed their profession and their responsibilities and they wonder why when Trump attacks them as hypocrites and overtly biased the crowds spontaneously and wildly cheer.

CHAPTER TWENTY-SEVEN
Media Collusion With the Clinton campaign

The WikiLeaks Podesta email dumps were particularly damaging to the Clinton campaign as well as the media because of the overwhelming and damning evidence of outright collusion between the nation's ostensibly impartial "arbiter" of news and the Clinton campaign. Numerous documented instances showed coordination between the Democratic Party, Clinton's campaign and the Washington press corps. Among some of the revelations: News organizations submitted stories to the Clinton campaign for approval prior to publication. Certain journalists began wearing their bias on their sleeves and were acknowledged as reliably pro-Hillary by the Clinton campaign.

CNN's Donna Brazille, submitted to the Clinton campaign two questions in advance, prior to a later scheduled Town Hall debate. CNBC/ New York Times contributor, John Harwood, prostrating himself before Podesta with unctuous flattery, giving the Clinton campaign unsolicited advice on how to deal with Trump. This is the same smarmy Harwood, who asked Trump at one of the Republican debates: "Let's be honest, is this a comic book version of a presidential campaign?" In a December 2015 email to Podesta, Harwood bragged about his much- criticized debate performance. Harwood titled the email "I imagine..." and continued the sentence in the body of the email, writing, "...that Obama feels some (sad) vindication at this demonstration of his years-long point about the opposition party veering off the rails.""I certainly am feeling that way with respect to how I questioned Trump at our debate." Harwood then bragged to Podesta about his pugnacious style. Harwood's conviviality is particularly odious, and he debased himself so thoroughly that it were as if he had said to the Clinton campaign: "Is there anything else I can do for you Hillary?"

Not to be outdone by his colleagues on the Hillary for President bandwagon, *Politico* reporter Glenn Thrush sent Podesta a chunk of his story-in-progress "to make sure I'm not fucking anything up." If there ever was any question as to the corruption of the media and their pretense of objectivity, the following instances of partiality and glaring conflicts of interest between members of the media and those in power for whom they are purportedly holding accountable.

In addition *Politico* chronicled more incidents of media cravenness: "In another email, The *Washington Post's* Juliet Eilperin offers Podesta a "heads up" about a story she's about to publish, providing a brief pre-publication synopsis. CNBC's Becky Quick promises to "defend" Obama appointee Sylvia Mathews Burwell. *New York Times* Magazine writer Mark Leibovich (who wrote a famous book lambasting permanent Washington's courtship rituals) asks Clinton's press secretary, Jennifer Palmieri, for permission to use portions of an off-the-record interview with the candidate. Palmieri withholds only a couple of comments and concludes her email to Leibovich, "Pleasure doing business!"

The WikiLeaks disclosures also were a stinging indictment of the media's utter lack of self-awareness concerning their inability to report the news impartially as well as their utter indifference for avoiding the appearance of impropriety. For example, Breitbart reported that:

[s]everal top journalists and television anchors RSVPed "yes" to attend a private off-the-record gathering at the home of Joel Beneson, the chief campaign strategist for Hillary Clinton, two days before she announced her candidacy for president. Breitbart noted the guest list for an early dinner event at the home of John Podesta in Washington was limited to reporters expected to cover Clinton on the campaign trail.

Among the media outlets compromised by being invited to dinner events with Podesta and other top Clinton aides were from NBC, ABC, CBS, CNN, MSNBC, CNBC the New York Times, the Washington Post, the

Wall Street Journal, the Daily Beast, the Los Angeles Times, McClatchy, People, the New Yorker, Bloomberg, Huffington Post, Buzzfeed, and Politico. Among the compromised journalists named were: Amy Chozick, Maggie Haberman, Jonathan Martin, Pat Healey, and Gail Collins of the New York Times, as well as George Stephanopoulos and Diane Sawyer of ABC. 75 "Leaked emails show that Hillary Clinton's campaign officials boasted about getting favorable news coverage from compliant journalists, received political advice from cozy reporters and circulated the names of journalists who were 'friendly' to the candidate," noted the Washington Times. "Whatever other revelations lurk in the huge cache of campaign emails being published by WikiLeaks, one thing is clear: Clinton campaign officials clearly exude an air of confidence that much of the mainstream media are in the bag for their candidate and hostile to Republican rival Donald Trump."[1]

Beyond WikiLeaks, a January 2015 Clinton strategy document obtained by the Intercept describes reporter Maggie Haberman—then at *Politico* and now at the New York Times—as someone the campaign "has a very good relationship with and who had been called upon to "tee up stories for us before" and had never disappointed.[2]

Additionally, "Among the most damaging contents of the WikiLeaks "Podesta Email File" were transcripts of the speeches Clinton gave to Goldman Sachs in 2013—Clinton had been paid as much as 225,000 dollars per speech—that contained statements so potentially damaging that Clinton had refused to release the transcripts when pressed to do so by Trump during the campaign. The speeches contained many compromising statements proving Clinton had supported Wall Street, both as US senator from New York, and as Secretary of State, and as a result enjoyed a high level of coziness with Wall Street top donors."[3]

CHAPTER TWENTY-EIGHT

Hillary's Health Coverup

During the election, the media had a predictable habit of acting remarkably docile when requested by the Clinton campaign. No better example of media malpractice, overt bias and obsequiousness suffices than the entire media's response to Hillary's collapsing insensate after a memorial service on 9/11 in the closing days of the campaign. Additionally, no incident better demonstrates the Clintons proclivity to lie and to lie profusely. For the fainting incident, the campaign's intentional cover-up strategy was straight from the 1990's Clinton scandal management playbook. Tell the big lie and when it's shown to be demonstrably false, lie again. Unfortunately for Hillary, that tactic by 2016 was shopworn, due to cell phone videos and mass distribution through alternative media channels like YouTube. The Clinton campaign was playing by rules that were no longer operative.

Questions were raised about Clinton's health ever since she suffered a serious concussion while Secretary of State in 2012. According to the FBI, when questioned about her lawless private email server, Hillary blamed the concussion for her alleged inability to recall specific details. In addition, journalists were well aware of her numerous coughing fits that occurred throughout the summer of 2016, including her uncontrolled fit during her labor day speech. As such, it was entirely reasonable to examine whether the affliction Clinton suffered previously in 2012 was still impacting her health — after all, it was Hillary who claimed the effects from her concussion prevented her from answering questions posed by the FBI with specificity. *Washington Post* columnist Chris Cilliza's response for those journalists who had the temerity in raising questions about the health of the likely first woman president, was typical of the indifference exhibited by the entire Mainstream Media-Democratic Party-Complex: "Can we just stop talking about Hillary Clinton's health now?"

Sean Davis, writing in *The Federalist* provides a synopsis of some of the headlines that captured the rough tenor of coverage of Hillary's health woes during the months of August and September, 2016:

CNN (Aug. 24, 2016): Clinton's health is fine, but what about Trump?
New York Post (Sept. 4, 2016): Dr. Drew loses show after discussing Hillary's health
Washington Post (Sept. 6, 2016): Can we just stop talking about Hillary Clinton's health now?
Sarah Silverman (Sept. 8, 2016): "I think anyone bringing up her health is a f***ing a**hole"[1]

Then, on September 11, 2016, Clinton was caught on camera seizing up and passing out as deadweight, appearing to be wracked by rigor mortis and then losing a shoe before being shoved into a waiting van. Suddenly, for those journalists, like Cilliza who had acted like lapdogs for the Clinton campaign, asking questions about Hillary's health, post-collapse, was no longer grounds for being banished from polite society. As Michael Goodwin writing in the *New York Post* observed: "Because they were scooped by the video, an army of journalists is now under pressure to report facts instead of covering them up.

Most important, voters got fresh proof that Clinton's first instinct is to lie, and then lie again."[2] Goodwin further notes that despite all knew of Clinton's natural instinct to lie, "... she humiliated the so-called best and brightest news organizations. Despite her unshakable reputation for being dishonest and untrustworthy, Clinton nonetheless managed to snooker most mainstream outlets into believing that her coughing fits were just allergies."

Clinton's collapse, ineradicably caught on video, precipitated, from Hillary's campaign, an entire series of material misrepresentations, easily debunked, that intentionally misstaed her condition and obscured the true reason for what ailed her the day she left the memorial service. In keeping with Hillary's demonstrated proficiency for pathological lying, each successive lie issued by the campaign could not be squared with the previous lie, never mind the damning and contradictory evidence of the public video of her dropping like an anchor at the door of her minivan. This was classic Clintonian deception.

The media's self-abasement and abrogation of their duty to report news stories accurately and diligently was particularly damning. The journalistic malpractice on display would have been embarrassing had the Mainstream Media-Democratic Party-Complex any shame or remorse for their dereliction of duty throughout the campaign. The refusal of the media to question the official spin given by the campaign for Hillary's fainting incident was particularly galling to ordinary voters because the veracity of their claims were easily refuted by their own subsequent statements, which in some cases were diametrically opposed to prior campaign pronouncements.

Larry O'Connor writing in *Hot Air* correctly noted the absurdity of the claims made by the Clinton campaign and the willingness of the press to accept as gospel, balderdash that was served up to them repeatedly: "What fact-based source was motivating journalists for the past several months to not only ignore the questions regarding Clinton's health, but, to aggressively and publicly shame and humiliate any reporter writing about their observations that, perhaps, Clinton was not the picture of health? The good word of the Clinton campaign and the candidate, herself.

That's right, the candidate with the lowest trustworthy ranking of any modern presidential candidate. The person known to skirt the truth if not lie outright on any issue that might make her or her husband look bad gave her own personal assurance to reporters that her health was fine.

And that was enough for them."[3] Wikileaks also demolished the myth that the media was an objective arbiter during the election. The incontrovertible evidence shows that not only was the press biased against Trump, they were openly assisting or colluding with the Clinton campaign.

PART SIX

REVENGE OF THE DEPLORABLES

CHAPTER TWENTY-NINE
Clinton Camp:Cautious Optimism

Shortly before the election, there was cautious optimism in the Clinton camp. As Allen and Parnes recall the mood of the campaign, "The early voting numbers in Florida were so good that even Bill Clinton, who had cared at Brooklyn's tendency to ignore his feel for politics on the ground, excitedly told one campaign aide that Friday before the election that the Sunshine State was in the bag. Furthermore, public polling showed Hillary with a clear lead nationally and in enough battleground states to carry the election with rooms to spare. The *New York Times'* Upshot, Nate Silver's FiveThirtyEight, and other election prognosticators related Hillary as the overwhelming favorite — though Silver's projection wasn't quite as rosy. By the time Comey returned to the spotlight two days before the election to say he still wouldn't recommend charges against Hillary, it was hard to find serious election analysts who were predicting a Trump victory."[1] We were feeling good about Florida, North Carolina, and Pennsylvania, said an aide who was traveling with Hillary. "We know we had taken a hit from Comey, but we didn't think it would be an insurmountable one. It was fun. There was an energy."[2]

Cautions optimism, as Allen and Parnes observed, seemed to prevail even to skeptics, "Everything Hilary was hearing and seeing pointed to a victory. Even Sullivan, the incorrigible pessimist, thought she was going to win in the final days. Nearly a decade after she'd launched her first campaign for the presidency, the glass ceiling was within Hilary's reach and the hammer of the American electorate was in her grasp."[3]

CHAPTER THIRTY
Election Night

For the Clinton team, November 7, 2016 was a heady day. In twenty-four hours, Hillary would be elected the first woman president of the United States. At the beginning of election night, the Javits Center was abuzz. "Supporters resplendent in their "I"m with Her" and "Madam President" T-shirts filed in and stood shoulder to shoulder as they watch the returns trickle in on the large television monitors overhead."[1] Allen and Parnes provide us a chronicle of how things went from bad to worse for Clinton on election night:

"About 9:30 p.m., one of Hillary's consultants sidled up next to spokesman Jesse Ferguson at a uruinal. The early numbers in Michigan looked so bad, the consultant said that Hillary was probably finished. On the convention hall floor, grown men and women groaned with each burst of additional bad news. Some cried. Others left early. The block party, once so boisterous, cleared out quickly, and a spillover room just off the stage never filled as aides had anticipated."[2]

"The torture was excruciating in large part because, while it was clear Trump was out performing expectations, the races in Pennsylvania, Michigan, and Wisconsin were too close to call definitively. They were all much worse for Hillary that her private modeling and public police had projected. It would take some time to figure out just how bad."[3]

Then, as Allen and Parnes write, they lost Wisconsin, " In the conference room next door, Hillary's "states" team — feeling track of the operations and results in each of the states — flipped the TV to the reviled Fox News Channel. The other networks simply weren't calling races as aggressively. At 11:30 p.m.,

Fox's Megan Kelly reported that Trump had won Wisconsin and, in the same breath, explained the real significance of the state's ten electoral voter: "There goes her blue wall."

Until that moment, most Democrats—including most of Hillary's team — believed that she would hold the states that Democrats had won in every election since 1992. Called the 'blue wall," these states accounted for all but twenty-eight of the electoral votes she would need to capture the presidency. None of the states she'd lost to that point — not Florida or North Carolina or Ohio — was part of the blue wall…A nation of Democrats sat in stunned silence. They hadn't been warned. Even her pollsters had even in the dark, sidelined in favor of an analytics team that insisted she was poised to win.[4]"

One by one, as the key states were called for Trump and the electoral votes tallied inexorably in his favor, the faces on the anchors, commentators and reporters were long and drawn out; shellshocked, they gazed into the camera, disbelief in their plaintive voices. They all spoke in hushed tones, as if they had just been notified that a close family member had died.

The reporters were all visibly weary from a long night of covering an election that every pundit, commentator and cable TV anchor thought was a foregone conclusion. No matter how some tried, it was impossible to hide their disbelief and sense of foreboding. Over at ABC News, reporter Martha Raddatz, who had clashed needlessly with Trump at the second presidential debate, began to cry.

Before the night was over, the explanations from many of these "expert" commentators began to trickle in: with nary a mention of the serial lies about her private email server, came the pronouncements spoken with certitude: obviously Hillary lost due to rampant misogony, among the bitter clingers; others blamed a dangerous emergence of white nationalism. Hillary's loss was a "whitelash" cried an unhinged Van Jones on CNN. This convoluted theory contends that even though Hillary wasn't an African American, the only explanation for her loss was that some of the same voters who voted for Obama twice, were now casting their ballots against the nations's first African-American president. Go figure...

True to form, MSNBC did not disappoint in their zeal to be the most stridently partisan. Rachel Maddow saw it as her sacred duty to warn her viewers of the apocalypse to come. What those watching television on election night witnessed was the complete meltdown of the mainstream media Democratic Party complex.

Here is Steve Schmidt, longtime Republican consultant, a veritable font of wisdom on election night, demonstrating why the Republican Party has been getting fleeced by its consultant class: "STEVE SCHMIDT:

When we, when we look at this-- When we look at where this race is today, the Presidential race is effectively over.

(OVERTALK)

STEVE SCHMIDT:

Hillary Rodham Clinton will be the 45th President of the United States. Chuck Schumer will be the Majority Leader of the United States Senate.

CHUCK TODD:

You're that confident?

STEVE SCHMIDT:

And the only question that's still up in the air is how close the Democrats will come to retaking the House Majority. What this exposes, though, is much deeper and it goes to the Republican Party as an institution. This, this candidacy, the magnitude of its disgrace to the country is almost impossible, I think, to articulate. But it has exposed the intellectual rot in the Republican Party. It has exposed at a massive level the hypocrisy, the modern day money changers in the temple like Jerry Falwell Jr. And so, this party, to go forward and to represent a conservative vision for America, has great soul searching to do. And what we've seen and the danger for all of these candidates is over the course of the last year, these, these candidates who have repeatedly put their party ahead of their country, denying what is so obviously clear to anybody who's watching about his complete and total manifest unfitness for this office.[5]

CHAPTER THIRTY-ONE

Au Revoir, Marie Antoinette

Through the WikiLeaks revelations and the manner in which Hillary conducted her campaign, the white working class learned that the elites of the Democratic Party were openly contemptuous of the concerns and cultural affinities of Middle America. The coal miners whom JFK had embraced were now told by Hillary that her party wanted them to lose their jobs — all in the name of saving the planet. Both prior to and during the election, the decimated working class of the heartland was lectured constantly by Democratic Party officials and their water carriers in the media that they would have to change their ways and lose their many deep-seated prejudices if they wanted to be part of this new coalition of the ascendant: dismantle their gun racks; stop thumping their bibles and understand, that despite their palpable suffering, they were the beneficiaries of "white privilege."

The "basket of deplorables" comment, which astonishingly Hillary refused to retract, was the breaking point for many middle class voters. Breathtakingly disdainful and injudicious as this statement may have been, it was merely the logical extension of Obama's "bitter clingers" commentary. While this phrase may have been music to the ears of Hillary's assembled crowd of rich elites, perhaps in retrospect, it wasn't a smart idea to bastardize, in one fell swoop, an entire swath of the electorate whose concerns Democrats had long pretended to embrace. The silent but proud irredeemables, tired of being mercilessly mocked by the party and its wholly owned subsidiary, the mainstream media, patiently waited for their chance to respond to Hillary's Marie Antoinette moment.

On November 8th, the peasants, some of whom had been lifetime Democrats, tired of being derided for their "whiteness", their racism and their rank stupidity, "stormed the Bastille" and denied her Highness another term at Versailles.

CHAPTER THIRTY-TWO
A Media Mea Culpa

During the election, media condescension towards Trump and his supporters was rampant. Here is how New Yorker, Matt Taibbi described Trump on a visit to Iowa on August 27, 2016. "The small traveling press corps following the candidate glibly files out of a shuttle van into "Joni's Roast n' Ride," which turns out to be a mud-floored barn packed with yet another whooping-and-hollering all-white crowd dressed in biker regalia, mesh hats and flag-themed shirts.

It's a hardcore audience. Imaging the set of Her Haw mixed with a Strom Thurmond rally, and you get the idea. If Colin Kaepernick walked in here by mistake, he would probably be skeletonize in seconds."[1]

After the election, a somewhat penitent Taibbi engages in a mea culpa when describing how his fellow cloistered and smug journalists completely missed the wave of discontent surging through Middle America that swept Trump into the White House. "The almost universal failure among political pros to predict Trump's victory — the few exceptions, conspicuously. Were people who hailed from rust-belt states, like Michael Moore — spoke to an astonishing cultural blindness. Those of us whose job it is to cover campaign long ago are accustomed to treating The People as a kind of dumb animal. Whose behavior could sometimes be unpredictable but, in the end, almost did what it was told.

Whenever we sought insight into the motives and tendencies of the elusive creature, our first calls were always to other eggheads like ourselves. We talked to pollsters, think-tanker, academics, former campaign strategists, party spokes-hacks, even the journalist. Day after day, our political talks shows consisted of one geek in a suit interviewing another geek in a suit about the behaviors of pope fitters and store clerks and cops in Florida, Wisconsin, Ohio and West Virginia. We'd stand over glitzy video maps and discuss demographic data pints like we were trying to determine the location of a downed jetliner."[2]

PART SEVEN

POSTSCRIPT

The Party of Martha's Vineyard

The contempt for which Hillary and the Democratic Party showed for those Trump supporters in flyover country, in conjunction with an ever-widening cultural divide between elites and voters, helps explain why Martha's Vineyard has been the preferred vacation destination for leaders of the new Democratic Party. A favorite of the Clintons and Obamas, this charming and picturesque island, by its geographical isolation, is very much secluded from the outside world. Although it is a mere forty-minute ferry ride from the Cape, the island is nonetheless quite remote from the mainland in terms of the cultural and socio-economic character of its residents. Opulence is rife on the Vineyard. John Kerry windsurfs nearby on Nantucket Sound. The wealthy residents live in their dwellings cloistered and secluded behind tall shrubs that act as walls separating them from the outside world and its inhabitants. As part of the Commonwealth of Massachusetts, the reigning political philosophy on the island is unabashed echo-chamber liberalism. It should come as no surprise that the Vineyard heartily welcomes Democratic presidents and party elites as rock stars.

Why don't Democrats favor Hyannisport, home of the Kennedy compound, as an alternate vacation destination? The allure of the Vineyard is just too strong. The island's exclusivity, elitism and the fabulous wealth of its many residents is more befitting for those who believe their self-sacrifice as "public servants" entitles them to live like royalty, with all its trappings and luxuriant splendor. Leaders of the party can enjoy the beneficence of the island's affluent patrons who are only too eager to turn over their multi-million dollar homes rent-free for the benefit of visiting Democratic presidents.

More importantly, since the Vineyard, but not the Cape, is a magnet for the fabulously wealthy, there would be no opportunity to golf with NBA stars, obscenely rich business moguls and various other elite one per center's. Long time Democratic Party fundraiser, serial groper, misogynist, and progressive icon Harvey Weinstein, is no stranger to the island, just ask Hillary Clinton, who on more than one occasion, has been the object of his campaign donation benefaction.

One must wonder, how much of the conversation between holes on the golf course is about the Presidents' guests paying their "fair share" in taxes. The upscale, and sequestered environment of the Vineyard, far from the apprehensions and concerns of most everyday Americans, is a perfect illustration on how the temperament of the modern day Democratic Party has been transformed.

Like the Democratic Party, Martha's Vineyard has changed. Once accessible to ordinary folks for a week's vacation in the summer, the island is now heavily populated with renowned Ivy League academics, Wall Street tycoons who fly in from New York City on their private jets, stars of the entertainment world and millionaires who reside in their splendid and lavish homes. For many middle class families, for whom a vacation is a luxury, visiting the Vineyard now is far beyond their reach. Everything on the island is expensive and establishments cater to the well to do. You won't find any Wal-Mart's, deplorables or Republicans here. In short, this is the perfect vacation spot for members of the new Democratic Party.

After the election, Democrats will have a grand time on the island with their Hollywood friends their smug, sanctimonious, urban elites and all the other 1 percenters, whom, despite being the objects of their phony vituperation, have always been part of their inner circle.

PART EIGHT

ENDNOTES

Prologue

[1] Robert W. Merry, "5 Reasons Trump Is Dominating American Politics", National Interest, May 29, 2016, http://nationalinterest.org/feature/5-reasons-trump-dominating-american-politics-16384?page=2

[2] Ibid

[3] Jim Geraghty, "The RNC's 2012 Autopsy Was Wrong", *National Review*, January 28, 2013, http://www.nationalreview.com/article/431001/rnc-2012-autopsy-wrong-immigration

[4] Heather MacDonald, "The Big Lie of the Anti-Cop Left Turns Lethal
The real story behind the murder of two NYPD officers", *City Journal*, December 22, 2014,

Chapter One

[1] Sean Trende, "Why Trump? Why Now?", January 29, 2016, http://www.realclearpolitics.com/articles/2016/01/29/why_trump_why_now_129486.html

[2] Ibid

[3] Robert W. Merry, "5 Reasons Trump Is Dominating American Politics", *National Interest*, May 29, 2016, http://nationalinterest.org/feature/5-reasons-trump-dominating-american-politics-16384?page=2

Chapter Two

[1] R.R. Reno, "What Trump Teaches Us", First Things, March 4, 2016, https://www.firstthings.com/featured-author/r-r-reno

* * *

Chapter Three

[1] Byron York, "GOP fear and loathing in New Hampshire", *Washington Examiner*, January 24, 2016, http://www.washingtonexaminer.com/byron-york-gop-fear-and-loathing-in-new-hampshire/article/2581329

[2] Ibid

[3] Ibid

[4] Ibid

[5] Richard Wolffe, "Win or lose, Republicans are heading for civil war after election day", *The Guardian*, November 7, 2016, https://www.theguardian.com/us-news/2016/nov/07/republicans-lose-election-day-donald-trump-civil-war

[6] Taylor Hiegel, "They shoot defeated political consultants, don't they?", *NBC News*, Mar 15, 2013, http://firstread.nbcnews.com/_news/2013/03/15/17328682-they-shoot-defeated-political-consultants-dont-they

Running off the same old playbook

[1] Jim Geraghty, "The RNC's 2012 Autopsy Was Wrong", *National Review*, February 8, 2016, http://www.nationalreview.com/article/431001/rnc-2012-autopsy-wrong-immigration

[2] Jim Geraghty, "The RNC's 2012 Autopsy Was Wrong", *National Review*, February 8, 2016, http://www.nationalreview.com/article/431001/rnc-2012-autopsy-wrong-immigration

[3] Jay Cost, "Republican Party Down", *The Weekly Standard*, May 09, 2016, http://www.weeklystandard.com/republican-party-down/article/2002180

[4] Ibid

Chapter Four

[1] Eli Stokols, Inside Jeb Bush's $150 Million Failure, Politico, February 20,2016,

http://http://www.politico.com/magazine/story/2016/02/jeb-bush-dropping-out-set-up-to-fail-213662

[2] Ibid.

[3] Ibid.

The Rip Van Winkle of the 2016 Election Cycle

[1] As quoted, "Bush believes in man-made global warming and wants plenty more of it", *American Thinker*, July 31, 2015

[2] Tim Alberta, "Jeb Bush and the Death of a Dynasty", *National Review*, February 21, 2016, http://www.nationalreview.com/article/431683/jeb-bush-campaign-obituary?target=topic&tid=1709

[3] Ibid

4   "Bush, Like GOP Reset Plan, Was Blindsided by Trump", Rebecca Berg, Real Clear Politics,

February 23, 2016,http://www.realclearpolitics.com/articles/2016/02/23/
bush_like_gop_reset_plan_was_blindsided_by_trump_129757.html

* * *

Chapter Five

1   Stone, Roger (2017-01-31). The Making of the President 2016: How Donald Trump Orchestrated a Revolution (Kindle Locations 793-805). Skyhorse Publishing. Kindle Edition.

2   Ibid

3   As quoted, Stone, Roger. The Making of the President 2016: How Donald Trump Orchestrated a Revolution (Kindle Locations 860-862). Skyhorse Publishing. Kindle Edition.

4   Rich Noyes, "Flashback: Journalists Mocked Trump's Announcement as a Joke", NewsBusters, http://www.newsbusters.org/blogs/nb/rich-noyes/2017/01/19/flashback-journalists-mocked-trumps-announcement-joke

5   As quoted, Stone, Roger (2017-01-31). The Making of the President 2016: How Donald Trump Orchestrated a Revolution (Kindle Locations 805-834). Skyhorse Publishing. Kindle Edition.

Trump attacks the Old Order

1   Ramesh Ponnuru, "Learning from Trump", National Review, August 12, 2016, http://www.nationalreview.com/article/438909/donald-trump-republican-party-conservatives-should-learn-his-candidacy

2   Jordan Carney, "'Circus' around immigration debate hurting GOP", The Hill, July 19, 2015, http://thehill.com/blogs/floor-action/senate/247574-mccain-circus-around-immigration-debate-hurting-gop

Trump Confronts confronts Media

1   "Trump Defiant After Reporter Says 'Anchor Baby' Is an Offensive Term", Fox News Insider, August 20, 2015, http://insider.foxnews.com/2015/08/20/video-donald-trump-anchor-baby-ill-still-say-it-even-if-its-not-politically-correct

Chapter Six

1   Jay Cost, "Why They Like Him", The Weekly Standard, August 10, 2015,http://www.weeklystandard.com/why-they-like-him/article/1001596

The rise of Trump

1   Mark Steyn, "Nitwits of the Round Table", Steyn Online, February 25, 2016, http://www.steynonline.com/7479/nitwits-of-the-round-table

2   Stone, Roger. The Making of the President 2016: How Donald Trump Orchestrated a Revolution (Kindle Locations 925-927). Skyhorse Publishing. Kindle Edition.

3   Ibid, (Kindle Location 1424).

Jeb struggles

[1] Ibid, (Kindle Locations 1085-1090).

[2] Tim Alberta, Jeb Bush and the Death of a Dynasty", National Review, February 21, 2016, http://www.nationalreview.com/article/431683/jeb-bush-campaign-obituary?target=topic&tid=1709

[3] Michael C. Bender and Mark Halperin, "Jeb Bush Orders Across-the-Board Pay Cuts for Struggling Campaign", http://www.bloomberg.com/news/articles/2015-10-23/jeb-bush-orders-across-the-board-pay-cuts-for-struggling-campaign

[4] Daniel Strauss and Alex Isenstadt, "Bush's Iowa performance is even worse than expected",http://www.politico.com/story/2016/02/jeb-bush-iowa-caucuses-218594

Autopsy Report Backfires

[1] Peter Spilakos, "The Permanent Revolt of the Republican Elites", National Review, July 7, 2016, http://www.nationalreview.com/postmodern-conservative/437607/permanent-revolt-republican-elites?target=topic&tid=1709

[2] Ibid

The collapse of Marco Rubio

[1] Michael Brendan Dougherty, "Is Donald Trump unbeatable?", The Week.com, February 21, 2016, http://theweek.com/articles/607356/donald-trump-unbeatable

The Gang of Eight betrayal

[1] Tony Blair: Against Populism, the Center Must Hold

Trump has a string of primary victories

[1] John O' Sullivan, "The Rise of the Undocumented Republicans", National Review, February 26, 2016, http://www.nationalreview.com/article/431951/donald-trump-gop-future

Establishment tries to stop

[1] Alexander Burns, Maggie Halberman and Jonathan Martin, "Inside the Republican Party's Desperate Mission to Stop Donald Trump", New York Times, February 27, 2016, http://www.nytimes.com/2016/02/28/us/politics/donald-trump-republican-party.html?ribbon-ad-idx=4&rref=collection/newseventcollection/election-2016

[2] Alexander Burns, Maggie Halberman and Jonathan Martin, "Inside the Republican Party's Desperate Mission to Stop Donald Trump", New York Times, February 27, 2016, http://www.nytimes.com/2016/02/28/us/politics/donald-trump-republican-party.html?ribbon-ad-idx=4&rref=collection/newseventcollection/election-2016

[3] Ibid

[4] John O' Sullivan, "Donald Trump & the GOP of the Future", National Review, http://www.nationalreview.com/article/431951/donald-trump-gop-future

Romney harshly criticizes

[1]   Byron York, "Showing strength in Michigan, Trump feeds on hostility to GOP, Romney" Washington Examiner, March 6, 2016, http://www.washingtonexaminer.com/byron-york-showing-strength-in-michigan-trump-feeds-on-hostility-to-gop-romney/article/2585106

* * *

And then there was one

[1]   Pat Buchanan, *An Establishment in Panic*, March 3, 2016, World Net Daily.com, http://www.wnd.com/2016/03/an-establishment-in-panic/

Trump attacks Hillary

[1]   Steve Holland and Valerie Volcovici, "Eyeing an Indiana victory, Trump says 'It's over,'" Reuters, May 2, 2016, http://www.reuters.com/ article/ us-usa-election-trump-idUSKCN0XS1AE.

Chapter Seven

[1]   Michael Barone, "Obama Will Leave the Democrats in Shambles", *Washington* Examiner, November 4, 2014, http://www.realclearpolitics.com/articles/2014/11/04/obama_will_leave_the_democrats_in_shambles_124554.html

[2]   Ibid

Chapter Nine

[1]   Jonathan Allen & Amy Parnes, "Shattered: Inside Hillary Clinton's Doomed Campaign", (New York: Crown Publishing, 2017), p.55

[2]   Ibid, p.61

[3]   As quoted: "Emails show close Clinton allies in dark, shocked over 'insane' server setup", *Fox News*, October 27, 2016, http://www.foxnews.com/politics/2016/10/27/emails-show-close-clinton-allies-in-dark-shocked-over-insane-server-setup.html

[4]   Jonathan Allen & Amy Parnes, "Shattered: Inside Hillary Clinton's Doomed Campaign", (New York: Crown Publishing, 2017), p.56

[5]   Ibid

Chapter Ten

[1]   Paul Sperry, "Meet the Mastermind Behind Clinton's Massive Email Coverup", *New York Post*, September 4, 2016, http://www.nypost.com/2016/09/04/meet-the-mastermind-behind-clintons-massive-email-coverup/

Chapter Eleven

[1]   Jonathan Allen & Amy Parnes, "Shattered: Inside Hillary Clinton's Doomed Campaign", (New York: Crown Publishing, 2017), p.54

[2]   Howard Kurtz, "Haunting Hillary: Why the email story is spinning out of control", *Fox News, http://www.foxnews.com/politics/2015/10/09/haunting-hillary-why-email-story-is-spinning-out-control.html*

[3]   Jonathan Allen & Amy Parnes, "Shattered: Inside Hillary Clinton's Doomed Campaign", (New York: Crown

Publishing, 2017), p.68

* * *

Chapter Twelve

1   Larry O' Connor, 8" Minutes Of Shame: Reporters Covering Hillary Embarrass Profession With Softball Questions", *Hot Air*, June 6, 2016, http://www.hotair.com/archives/2016/06/06/8-minutes-of-shame-reporters-covering-hillary-embarrass-profession-with-softball-questions/

2   Elizabeth Harrington, "Clinton Campaign Boasts About Media: 'Every Single Interviewer Was for Her'", *Washington Free Beacon*, October 11, 2016, http://www.freebeacon.com/politics/clinton-campaign-boasts-media-every-single-interviewer/

3   "Clinton Email Scandal: How A Biased Press Tried To Ignore It | Stock News & Stock Market Analysis", *Investors Business Daily*, March 28, 2016, http://www.investors.com/politics/editorials/clinton-email-scandal-how-a-biased-press-tried-to-ignore-it/

Chapter Thirteen

1   Jonathan Allen & Amy Parnes, "Shattered: Inside Hillary Clinton's Doomed Campaign", (New York: Crown Publishing, 2017)

2   Stone, Roger. The Making of the President 2016: How Donald Trump Orchestrated a Revolution (Kindle Locations 5946-5957). Skyhorse Publishing. Kindle Edition.

Chapter Fourteen

1   Jonathan Allen & Amy Parnes, "Shattered: Inside Hillary Clinton's Doomed Campaign", (New York: Crown Publishing, 2017), p.113

2   8 minutes of shame: Reporters covering Hillary embarrass profession with softball questions, Larry O'Connor, June 6, 2016

, *Hot Air*,http://hotair.com/archives/2016/06/06/8-minutes-of-shame-reporters-covering-hillary-embarrass-profession-with-softball-questions/

3   Jonathan Allen & Amy Parnes, "Shattered: Inside Hillary Clinton's Doomed Campaign", (New York: Crown Publishing, 2017), p.132

4   Ibid, p.137

5   Ibid, p.137

6   Ibid, p.138

7   Ibid, p.136

8   Ibid, p.153

9   Ibid, p.177

10   Ibid, p.178

11   Jonathan Allen & Amy Parnes, "Shattered: Inside Hillary Clinton's Doomed Campaign", (New York: Crown Publishing, 2017), p.178

12   Jonathan Allen & Amy Parnes, "Shattered: Inside Hillary Clinton's Doomed Campaign", (New York: Crown

Publishing, 2017), p.178

[13]   Ibid, p.219

* * *

Chapter Fifteen

[1]   Kimberley A. Strassel, "The Press Buries Hillary Clinton's Sins", *Wall Street Journal*, October 13, 2016, http://www.wsj.com/articles/the-press-buries-hillary-clintons-sins-1476401308

[2]   Matt Welch, "Admit it, Dems: Hillary Could Strangle a Puppy on Live TV, and You'd Still Back Her", http://www.reason.com/blog/2015/07/24/admit-it-dems-hillary-could-strangle-a-p

Chapter Sixteen

[1]   Jonathan Allen & Amy Parnes, "Shattered: Inside Hillary Clinton's Doomed Campaign", (New York: Crown Publishing, 2017), p.313

[2]   Ibid,, p 397

Make the election contest all about Trump

[1]   Stone, Roger. The Making of the President 2016: How Donald Trump Orchestrated a Revolution (Kindle Locations 5209-5212). Skyhorse Publishing. Kindle Edition.

[2]   Becket Adams, 'We're done': CNN cuts off conservative guest's microphone", *Washington Examiner*, December 22, 2015, http://www.washingtonexaminer.com/were-done-cnn-cuts-off-conservative-guests-microphone/article/2578958

[3]   Mollie Hemingway, "Donald Trump Is Smart To Remind Voters Of Clinton Drama" *The Federalist, http://www.thefederalist.com/2015/12/31/donald-trump-is-smart-to-remind-voters-of-clinton-drama/*

Chapter Seventeen

[1]   Dan Metcalfe, "Hillary's email Defense is Laughable", *Politico*, March 16, 2015, http://www.politico.com/magazine/story/2015/03/hillary-clinton-email-scandal-defense-laughable-foia-116116#.VQgdWBDF8ex

[2]   Ibid

[3]   Ibid

Chapter Eighteen

[1]   Rosalind S. Helderman, Tom Hamburger and Steven Rich, "Clintons' foundation has raised nearly $2 billion — and some key questions", February 18, 2015, http://www.washingtonpost.com/politics/clintons-raised-nearly-2-billion-for-foundation-since-2001/2015/02/18/b8425d88-a7cd-11e4-a7c2-03d37af98440_story.html?utm_term=.79c9b853985d

[2]   Rick Cohen, "The Philanthropic Problem with Hillary Clinton's Huge Speaking Fees", Non Profit Quarterly, July 11, 2014, http://www.archive.is/20160531180504/https://nonprofitquarterly.org/2014/07/11/the-philanthropic-problem-with-hillary-clinton-s-huge-speaking-fees/#selection-1145.0-1145.67

[3]   Aaron Klein, "Hillary Appointed Clinton Foundation Donor, Financial Bundler to Sensitive Intel Post", Breitbart, June 11,2016, http://www.breitbart.com/2016-presidential-race/2016/06/11/hillary-appointed-clinton-

foundation-donor-financial-bundler-sensitive-intel-post/

[4] Elise Jordan, "Hillary Clinton's Reaction to Her Foundation Scandal Is Disastrous", *Time*, August 25, 2016, http://www.time.com/4466911/hillary-clinton-email-excuses/

[5] Ibid

[6] Michael Walsh, "How corporate America bought Hillary Clinton for $21M", *New York Post*, May 22, 2016, http://www.nypost.com/2016/05/22/how-corporate-america-bought-hillary-clinton-for-21m/

[7] Benjamin Bell, "Robert Reich Still Sees No 'Convincing Explanation' on Hillary Clinton Email", *ABC News*, June 5, 2015, http://web.archive.org/web/20160322035147/http://abcnews.go.com/Politics/robert-reich-sees-convincing-explanation-hillary-clinton-email/story?id=31550795

[8] Curtis Houck, "Networks Ignore Clinton E-Mail Scandal; ABC and NBC Skip Clinton Foundation Controversy", *Newsbusters*, March 15, 2015, http://www.newsbusters.org/blogs/curtis-houck/2015/03/16/networks-ignore-clinton-e-mail-scandal-abc-and-nbc-skip-clinton

[9] Scott McCay, "Rotten to the Core", *The American Spectator*, October 25, 2016, http://spectator.org/rotten-to-the-core/

[10] Ibid

[11] Ibid

[12] Ibid

[13] Deroy Murdock, "The Clintons and their minions deserve to be driven from public life", National Review, November 5, 2016, http://www.nationalreview.com/article/441819/hillary-clinton-bill-clinton-corruption-flush-toilet

[14] Conor Friedersdorf, "Clinton's Flaws Simply Aren't Comparable to Trump's", *The Atlantic*, Nvember 1, 2016, http://www.theatlantic.com/author/conor-friedersdorf/

[15] Ibid

[16] Ibid

[17] Ibid

[18] Ibids

Chapter Twenty

[1] Holman W. Jenkins, Jr.., "Hillary Clinton Becomes the Unsafe Hand", *Wall Street Journal*, November 1, 2016, http://www.wsj.com/articles/hillary-clinton-becomes-the-unsafe-hand-1478042102

[2] Rich Lowry, "Hillary still can't explain why she should be president", *New York Post*, *May 23, 2016*, http://nypost.com/2016/05/23/hillary-still-cant-explain-why-she-should-be-president/

Chapter Twenty-Two

[1] Jonathan Allen & Amy Parnes, "Shattered: Inside Hillary Clinton's Doomed Campaign", (New York: Crown Publishing, 2017), p.315`

[2] Ibid

[3]   Ibid

[4]   Ibid., p.316

* * *

Trump a different kind of Republican

[1]   Kimberley A. Strassel, "Trump Rakes the Clinton Muck", *Wall Street Journal*, May 26, 2016, http://www.wsj.com/articles/trump-rakes-the-clinton-muck-1464302380?cb=logged0.786307911388576

Attacks media as corrupt

[1]   Dylan Byers and Jeremy Diamond, "Donald Trump's 'sleaze' attack on reporter hits new level of media animosity", *CNN*, May 31, 2016, http://money.cnn.com/2016/05/31/media/donald-trump-reporter-sleaze/index.html

[2]   Jeremy Diamond, "Donald Trump launches all-out attack on the press", *CNN*, http://www.cnn.com/2016/05/31/politics/donald-trump-veterans-announcement/index.html

[3]   Ibid

[4]   Dylan Byers and Jeremy Diamond, "Donald Trump's 'sleaze' attack on reporter hits new level of media animosity", *CNN*, May 31, 2016, http://money.cnn.com/2016/05/31/media/donald-trump-reporter-sleaze/index.html

[5]   Cathy Burke, "Trump Vows to 'Punch Through' 'Dishonest' Media", *Newsmax*, August 1, 2016, http://www.newsmax.com/Politics/donald-trump-punch-through-dishonest/2016/08/01/id/741658/

[6]   Ibid

Attacks Hillary's Private Email Server

[1]   Jake Miller, "Donald Trump: Hillary Clinton guilty of "stupidity" on email server", *CBS News*, June 3, 2016, http://www.cbsnews.com/news/donald-trump-hillary-clinton-guilty-of-stupidity-on-email-server/

[2]   Justin Fishel, "Donald Trump Attacks Hillary Clinton After More Emails Released", August 10, 2016, http://abcnews.go.com/Politics/donald-trump-attacks-hillary-clinton-emails-released/story?id=41257876

[3]   Jose a. DelReal, John Wagner, Sean Sullivan, "As Clinton avoids talking about emails on campaign trail, Trump ramps up http://www.chicagotribune.com/news/nationworld/politics/ct-clinton-trump-campaign-20161030-story.html

Chapter Twenty-Four

[1]   As quoted, Eli Stokols, "The Bush Family's Lament", *Politico*, September 21, 2016, http://www.politico.com/story/2016/09/bush-family-donald-trump-228446

[2]   Victor Davis Hanson, "The Case for Trump", *National Review*, October 17, 2016, http://www.nationalreview.com/article/441126/donald-trump-conservatives-should-vote-president

[3]   As quoted, Steve Benen, "RNC 'autopsy' co-author gives up on the Republican Party", *MSNBC*, August 1, 2016, http://www.msnbc.com/byline/steve-benen

[4]   Ibid

[5] Ibid.

[6] Michael Gerson, "Trump's angry white men", *The Washington Post*, October 3, 2016, http://
www.washingtonpost.com/opinions/trumps-angry-white-men/
2016/10/03/32af5f4e-898b-11e6-875e-2c1bfe943b66_story.html?utm_term=.1c175c383351#comments

[7] Michael Gerson, "A Politician -- and a Party -- Deserving of Contempt", *Real Clear Politics*", October 10, 2016,
http://www.realclearpolitics.com/articles/2016/10/10/a_politician_--_and_a_party_--
_deserving_of_contempt_132023.html

[8] Ibid

[9] Ibid

Impact of Tapes

[1] Dara Linddara, "Poll: Vast majority of Republican voters don't care much about the leaked Trump tape", *Vox*,
October 9, 2016, http://www.vox.com/2016/10/9/13217158/polls-donald-trump-assault-tape

[2] Ibid

Double Standards and Hypocrisy

[1] Victor Davis Hanson, "Trump: A Bogeyman or Just a Man?", National Review, March 15, 2016, http://
www.nationalreview.com/article/432786/trump-compared-to-obama-clintons

[2] Victor Davis Hanson, "Donald Trump: Conservatives Should Vote for Him for President", *National Review*,
October 17, 2016, http://www.nationalreview.com/article/441126/donald-trump-conservatives-should-vote-
president

Chapter Twenty-Five

[1] As quoted, Stone, Roger. The Making of the President 2016: How Donald Trump Orchestrated a Revolution
(Kindle Locations 4712-4717). Skyhorse Publishing. Kindle Edition

[2] Stone, Roger. The Making of the President 2016: How Donald Trump Orchestrated a Revolution (Kindle
Locations 4737-4744). Skyhorse Publishing. Kindle Edition.

[3] Alex Burns and Matt Flegenheimer, "Did You Miss the Presidential Debate? Here Are the Highlights," *New York
Times*, September 26, 2016, http://www.nytimes.com/ 2016/ 09/ 26/ us/ politics/ presidential-debate.html.

[4] As quoted, Stone, Roger. The Making of the President 2016: How Donald Trump Orchestrated a Revolution
(Kindle Locations 4984-4987). Skyhorse Publishing. Kindle Edition.

[5] Ibid

[6] Jonathan Allen & Amy Parnes, "Shattered: Inside Hillary Clinton's Doomed Campaign", (New York: Crown
Publishing, 2017), p.353

[7] Stone, Roger. "The Making of the President 2016: How Donald Trump Orchestrated a Revolution" (Kindle
Locations 5077). Skyhorse Publishing. Kindle Edition.

[8] Jonathan Allen & Amy Parnes, "Shattered: Inside Hillary Clinton's Doomed Campaign", (New York: Crown
Publishing, 2017), p.353

9   Stone, Roger. The Making of the President 2016: How Donald Trump Orchestrated a Revolution (Kindle Locations 5167-5168). Skyhorse Publishing. Kindle Edition.

10   Ibid

11   Ibid

12   As quoted, David P. Goldman, "Trump Will Win the National Battle for Legitimacy", *PJ Media*, October 9, 2016,

http://pjmedia.com/spengler/2016/10/09/trump-will-win-the-national-battle-for-legitimacy/

13   Jonathan Allen & Amy Parnes, "Shattered: Inside Hillary Clinton's Doomed Campaign", (New York: Crown Publishing, 2017), p.353

Chapter Twenty-Six

1   Justin Raimondo, "To fight Trump, journalists have dispensed with objectivity", *Los Angeles Times*, August 2, 2016, http://www.latimes.com/opinion/op-ed/la-oe-raimondo-trump-media-bias-20160802-snap-story.html

2   Ibid

Chapter Twenty-Seven

1   Ezra Dulis, "Wikileaks: Journalists Dined at Top Clinton Staffers' Homes Days Before Hillary's Campaign Launch", *Breitbart*, October 17, 2016, http://www.breitbart.com/big-journalism/2016/10/17/wikileaks-journalists-clinton-staff-homes-before-hillarys-campaign-launch/

2   Stone, Roger. The Making of the President 2016: How Donald Trump Orchestrated a Revolution (Kindle Locations 5252-5253). Skyhorse Publishing. Kindle Edition.

3   Stone, Roger. The Making of the President 2016: How Donald Trump Orchestrated a Revolution (Kindle Locations 5252-5253). Skyhorse Publishing. Kindle Edition.

Chapter Twenty-Eight

1   As quoted, Sean Davis, "Hillary Clinton's Campaign Needs To Hire Better Liars" *The Federalist*, September 12, 2016, http://thefederalist.com/2016/09/12/hillary-clintons-campaign-needs-hire-better-liars/

2   Michael Goodwin, "Hillary collapse coverage reveals absurdity of biased media", *New York Post*, September 14, 2016, http://nypost.com/2016/09/14/hillary-collapse-coverage-reveals-absurdity-of-biased-media/

3   Larry O'Connor, "How the media failed America with the #HillarysHealth story", *Hot Air*, September 12, 2016, https://hotair.com/archives/2016/09/12/media-failed-america-hillaryshealth-story/

Chapter Twenty-Nine

1   Jonathan Allen & Amy Parnes, "Shattered: Inside Hillary Clinton's Doomed Campaign", (New York: Crown Publishing, 2017), p.369

2   Ibid

3   Ibid, p.370

Chapter Thirty

[1]   Jonathan Allen & Amy Parnes, "Shattered: Inside Hillary Clinton's Doomed Campaign", (New York: Crown Publishing, 2017), p.375

[2]   Ibid, p.380

[3]   Ibid

[4]   Jonathan Allen & Amy Parnes, "Shattered: Inside Hillary Clinton's Doomed Campaign", (New York: Crown Publishing, 2017), p.381

[5]   "Meet the Press", October 9, 2016, *NBC News*, http://www.nbcnews.com/meet-the-press/meet-press-october-9-2016-n662746

Chapter Thirty-Two

[1]   Matt Taibbi, "Insane Clown President: Dispatches from the 2016 Circus" (New York) Spiegel & Grau, 2017, p.245

[2]   Ibid, p.282

Manufactured by Amazon.ca
Acheson, AB